GREAT GOURMET DISHES!

EXCITING, GRATIFYING,
SUPERLATIVE, REWARDING
are the words for this wonderful book
which will put new fragrance and flavor
into your cooking!

You can surprise and delight your
family and friends with rare and
succulent meals that can even be
served to children, since when wine
is cooked it contains no alcohol—
but serves to enhance and enrich the
flavor of fine food.

Myra Waldo, food consultant to Pan
American Airways, world traveler, and
author of numerous cook books, here gives
you all kinds of ways to increase the pleasures
of your table!

THE COMPLETE BOOK OF WINE COOKERY

BY MYRA WALDO

BANTAM BOOKS · TORONTO · NEW YORK · LONDON

THE COMPLETE BOOK OF WINE COOKERY

A Bantam Cookbook Shelf edition / published October 1965
2nd printing
3rd printing
4th printing

Library of Congress Catalog Card Number: 65-11849

Published simultaneously in the United States and Canada.

Bantam Books are published by Bantam Books, Inc., a subsidiary
of Grosset & Dunlap, Inc. Its trade-mark, consisting of the words
"Bantam Books" and the portrayal of a bantam, is registered in the
United States Patent Office and in other countries. Marca Registrada.
Bantam Books, Inc., 271 Madison Avenue, New York, N. Y. 10016.

PRINTED IN THE UNITED STATES OF AMERICA

Contents

Introduction	1
Appetizers	13
Soup	26
Fish	38
Poultry	59
Meat	95
Vegetables	162
Sauces and Dressings	171
Desserts	182
Index	191

Introduction

A half century ago, comparatively few Americans traveled abroad, but in the past decade, hundreds of thousands have toured Europe. At first, they visited only the capital cities; later, American tourists hired autos and drove through the smallest villages and hamlets of each country, exploring, sightseeing, eating the local dishes and drinking the local wines as they went. Once home, they missed having wine with their meals in the European style, and also yearned for the more sophisticated taste of foods prepared with wine.

Thus, the past several years have seen a tremendous surge of interest in this country in gourmet cooking, particularly in foreign dishes, and in wine-drinking. Not so very long ago, a guest invited to someone's home for dinner could expect either roast beef or turkey for the main course; if any alcoholic beverage was offered with the meal, it would probably be beer. But time brings changes, and Americans have become increasingly sophisticated in the matter of food and drink. Instead of a hackneyed, oft-repeated main course, guests are offered *coq au vin rouge* (chicken in red wine), *canard aux olives* (duck with olives), or *boeuf Bourguignonne* (beef in red wine). On the majority of occasions, the host will offer wine to his guests. Not infrequently, the host or hostess will remark that they first discovered the wine at a small country inn while touring France, Italy, or Spain, and how much they enjoyed it.

That is how the pattern began, how it continued and developed. First, Americans toured Europe and drank the local wine and ate the local cuisine. Once home, they sought out cook books with foreign recipes, and searched the liquor stores for their favorite wines. Foreign dishes and wines were served to their guests, and thus more and more people were exposed to European cooking and wines. Americans have responded with enthusiasm, as evidenced

1

by the rapidly mounting sales of wines, and cook books with foreign recipes.

What is wine, and what purpose does it serve? It is a completely natural beverage, being made from the juice of crushed grapes. There are hundreds of different kinds of grapes, grown in different countries, under many varied climatic conditions, and picked and processed by thousands of vintners; it is this variation in the end product that makes wines so fascinating, because there are literally thousands of different types. Wine originated many thousands of years ago, perhaps back in prehistoric times. In any event, the Bible speaks of it as a well-loved, familiar part of daily life. Water was often unsafe to drink, and wine was always pure, so it was only natural for wine to supplant water as a regular beverage. Over and above the safety factor of wine as opposed to water, was the fact that wine offered a special and rather delicious taste. In most parts of the world today the danger of contaminated water has decreased, and indeed has largely disappeared, but the popularity of wine continues unabated, and has increased steadily. Without doubt, it is the taste of wine that accounts for its public acceptance.

The remarkable thing about wine is that it actually improves the taste of food, and a co-relationship has been built up between food and wine over more than a thousand years. A delicious, skillful creation of a talented chef may have a superb taste; a fine bottle of wine may also, in its own way, have a superb taste. Peculiarly enough, the two together create a sort of harmony of flavors that makes both the dish and the wine taste even better than either does alone. Why this should be so is difficult to explain, but the "marriage" of tastes works to the advantage of both the food and wine. Furthermore, a mediocre dish may often be raised to a remarkably fine-tasting preparation by the addition of wine, for just as a glass of wine improves the taste of food, so does wine used in cooking improve the dish.

Many people are hesitant about ordering wine, being fearful of ordering the wrong wine with the wrong food. So much has been written about wine-drinking, and about the lore of wine, that many people assume that it is a difficult, perhaps esoteric science, which can be learned only after many years of apprenticeship. This is far from accurate, and anyone can become knowledgeable about the correct wines with the correct foods in a matter of minutes. Needless to say, becoming an authority on the subject of wines requires years of practice and a sensitive palate. But enjoying wines — that is something completely different. That comes almost immediately.

Inasmuch as wines have been drunk with meals for thousands of years, it is only natural that certain opinions have developed about what wines are most suited with certain foods. First, sweet dessert wines have been excluded from the category of table wines, because these are cloying and rich, and would spoil the taste of the food (this excludes port, Madeira, Marsala, and other sweet wines), although these wines may be used in cooking. The only wines to be served with food are the non-sweet type; the word "dry" is often used to describe these unsweetened wines, because they leave a sort of "dry" taste in the mouth and because they are low in sugar. At first taste, unaccompanied by food, a dry wine may seem a trifle displeasing to the palate; when taken with food, its dry quality will soon be found to enhance the natural taste of the particular food.

Over the years, a few basic principles have evolved, first and foremost of which is this simple basic premise: white wines with fish, red wines with meat. That simple fact is easily remembered, because the colors roughly match; most fish dishes are whitish, and most meats are red, and so are the wines that best accompany them. No one need be an absolute conformist, and if you wish to drink a white wine with red meat, that is your privilege. But first, everyone should at least try the combinations suggested by the mass of opinion accumulated by literally millions of wine-drinkers over thousands of years.

That simple rule of white wines with fish and red wines with meat can be readily applied, but a few exceptions come to mind. Certain meats are classifiable as white meats (when cooked), such as veal and pork; with these "white" meats, you could enjoy equally a red or a white wine. The same rule applies to chicken, with which either white or red wine is suitable. With duck or goose, however, a red wine is far better than a white. Also, cheese is always better with a red wine than with a white, and the same applies to spaghetti or *pasta* dishes, except when the *pasta* is served with a fish sauce, in which case a white wine would be more suitable.

There has been a geat deal of discussion about "vintage" wines. A vintage wine is the product of a particular year, and is referred to, for example, as the vintage of 1959. Americans are inclined to place unwarranted emphasis upon vintages; they often forget that even in good years, some bad wine is produced. On the other side of the coin, some good wine is produced even in years of a poor vintage.

Wines should be served at appropriate temperatures. White wines are always chilled; about three (or more) hours in a refrigerator will be sufficient. This is true except for champagne: because of its thick bottle, champagne requires almost six hours. If you are fortunate enough to own a wine bucket, fill it with plenty of ice cubes and cold water and revolve the wine bottle in it a few times; the intense cold will chill it in a matter of twenty to thirty minutes. White wines need not be opened until you are ready to serve them.

Red wines are different. First, they are served at what is called "room temperature"; however, the room temperature is that of a European home, where even today, central heating is not common. European room temperature means about 60-65°, not the 70° or more of American steam-heated homes. Red wines may be brought to correct temperature (if your home is warmer) by placing them briefly in the refrigerator (not more than twenty minutes), which will cool them slightly. Although white wines do not have to be opened in advance, red wines are best when the cork is removed about two hours before serving time. This allows the wines to "breathe," that is, to take in air. Because red wines have a heavier body than white wines, it is desirable that a little air be allowed to enter the freshly opened bottle, resulting in an improved taste. However, the earlier opening of red wines is not essential, but it does give additional quality.

Wine glasses should, wherever possible, be made of thin clear glass; thick glass is unpleasant to use and is not very esthetic. In the not very distant past, there were special wine glasses for every different wine, but in these days of limited domestic help and lack of storage space, only two principal types of glasses for wine remain. The red-wine glass is a fairly large, bowl-shaped glass (about the size and shape of a small orange) on a thin stem; the white-wine glass is a smaller version, about half the size of the red-wine glass. If you wish, only one type of wine glass need be used, but this should be the red-wine glass, which can also be used for white wines. On the other hand, the white-wine glass would be too small for the red wine, which needs room to "breathe." White-wine glasses should be half-filled, but red-wine glasses should not be filled more than one-third.

If there is any left-over wine, it may keep for a day or so, providing the bottle is promptly corked and placed in the refrigerator. Left-over red wine should, of course, be removed from the refrigerator the following day about two hours before serving time, to allow it to come to "room temperature." It is rare for an opened bottle of wine to keep for more than a day; after that, it will turn sour, and should not be drunk, or used in cooking. Don't open too much wine; the average bottle holds enough to serve 6-8 people with one glass each, but most people drink about two glasses with a meal. For a dinner party of 6-8 people, allow two bottles of wine.

Wines are produced on every continent of the world, although Asia accounts for the least. Wine production on a large scale is carried on, however, in Europe, Africa, North and South America, and Australia. Europe was and still is the center of the wine trade, and France produces the greatest variety of any country in the world. It is to France that everyone turns for any comparisons on production, types, tastes, and kinds of wine.

The two principal wine regions of France are Bordeaux and Burgundy. Considering Bordeaux first, this region lies in the southwestern part of the country, adjacent to the Atlantic Ocean, in a rather dreary, flat region. Bordeaux produces many of the finest wines in the world, and in addition a fair proportion of rather mediocre table wines, called *vin ordinaire* in France. The red wines of Bordeaux vary from a pale red to a very deep shade, and from a light body to a medium-heavy body. The white wines are somewhat less distinguished, except for a group of dessert wines, sweet and rich, the Sauternes. The table white wines are pleasant, but not very important. The Bordeaux region is subdivided into five principal districts — Pomerol, Médoc, Saint-Emilion, Graves, and Sauternes. In the year 1855, the wines of two of these districts — Médoc and Sauternes — were classified by the *Syndicat des Courtiers,* the Society of Wine Brokers. They found four wines to be outstanding — Château Lafite-Rothschild, Margaux, Latour, and Haut-Brion. They omitted from their list the highly regarded wine of Mouton-Rothschild, placing it at the head of the second category. The canny wine brokers of 1855 have been proven substantially correct, because for more than a century these five wines have been excellent wines (with the exception of some poor years), and have commanded the highest prices. Mouton-Rothschild should have been included in the first rank, and the fact that even today it often is in the greatest demand of any of the five helps to prove the point. However, only millionaires could afford to drink these wines regularly; their price is inevitably high. Other excellent and less expensive wines of Bordeaux that have come to the fore include Leoville-Poyferre, Rauzan-Gassies, Rausan-Segla, Gruaud-Larose, Pichon-Longueville, Palmer, Calon-Segur, Talbot, Beychevelle, Pontet-Canet, Lynch-Bages, and Mouton-d'Armailhacq.

In Bordeaux, grapes are grown on large tracts of land popularly called châteaux, because originally the lord of the region lived in a large mansion, or château. The name of the château—such as Château Margaux, for example — is a complete assurance that all of the wine sold under that label has been cultivated, harvested, processed, and bottled by the same firm. This is not true in Burgundy, where large châteaux are unknown. For one thing, a much smaller amount of land is involved. Furthermore, under the French law of inheritance, children are entitled to inherit equal shares in the property of their father. Therefore, when the owner of a vineyard dies, if he has three children, each inherits a one-third interest in the vineyard, and when the original owner's grandsons ultimately inherit their parents' shares there will often be still further division. This is not the situation in Bordeaux, where large vineyards are owned by powerful syndicates with a perpetual, corporate-type existence.

Burgundy, France's other great wine region, lies southeast of Paris and stretches from Dijon south to Lyons. In this comparatively small area, several of the world's great red wines (and at least one truly great white wine) are produced. The grapes grow in a narrow strip, less than a mile wide and extending for only 36 miles, and the countryside consists of a range of gentle slopes, which furnished this smiling land with its secondary name, the Cote d'Or, or Slopes of Gold. The average altitude of the better vineyards is about 800 feet; wine grapes grown on lower or higher altitudes are quite inferior.

Frenchmen, more than almost any other nationality, are extremely individualistic, and like to do things in their own particular way. For this reason, even though a vineyard name appears on a bottle of Burgundy, if several different firms processed the wine it is often (in fact usually) different from another similarly named bottle, even though both bear the same name. In some extreme cases, where there were a dozen different owners of the same vineyard, there were twelve quite different products. Some of the great red wines produced in Burgundy include Chambertin, Musigny, Clos Vougeot, Romanee-Conti, Echezaux, Nuits-St.-Georges, Pommard, and Volnay. The great white wine of Burgundy, perhaps the finest in the world, is Montrachet, a wine of great delicacy, flavor, and aroma.

One wine deserves some special mention, Beaujolais. It is produced just north of the city of Lyons, in the direction of Macon. The wine is made chiefly from the Gamay grape, one known for its high production, but not for its quality. The resulting wine is comparatively low in price, has a fruity taste, and is quite delicious to drink, but lacks subtlety. Of all red wines, it is perhaps one of the best for those who wish to become acquainted with wines at moderate cost. Also noteworthy is Chablis, a rather good white wine produced about eighty miles to the northwest of Dijon.

Another important wine region of France is the Rhone Valley, extending southward from Lyons to Avignon, over 1,000 miles. Both red and white wines are produced here, but the reds are better known. Like the Beaujolais, they have a pleasing quality, but are seldom important and are lower in price than most wines of Bordeaux and Burgundy. The three great names here are Hermitage, Cote-Rotie, and Chateauneuf-du-Pape.

There are other wines produced all over France — for example, the light wines of the Loire Valley, the fruity wines of Alsace, and especially the most publicized wine in the world — champagne. Champagne is a white wine made from both black and white grapes, which are so treated and processed as to result in a pale gold wine, sparkling and delightful. Many people say that champagne may be drunk with fish, meat, or dessert. But I think that champagne is not very good with meat, and I do not recommend it. Champagnes are prepared in five principal types, for various tastes and markets. *Brut* contains ½ to 1% of sugar; *Extra Dry,* or *Extra Sec,* contains from 1 to 2%; *Sec,* or *Dry,* has from 3 to 6%; *Demi-Sec* contains from 7 to 10%, and *Doux* has 10 to 15%.

German wines are not in the same class with those of France for sheer variety, but German wines include some of the finest and most expensive in the world. Germany, however, has no good red wine, in fact not even a passable one; its fame rests exclusively with its white wines. The German white wines tend to have a flowery bouquet, a low alcoholic content, and a most attractive light gold color, with a somewhat greenish undertone.

The wine region of Germany is located in the western part of the country, a comparatively short distance to the east of the French province of Alsace. It is quite far north, and this factor hinders large-scale wine production, but often results in some extraordinarily fine vintages. The most important wines are produced in two river valleys — the Rhine and the Moselle.

Because this region is well to the north, away from the hot sunshine of the south, the grapes often do not have sufficient sunshine to permit them to mature properly. For this reason, while the ordinary harvest time in France is late September or early October, in Germany it does not come until the middle of October, and this brings with it the ever-present danger of sudden frost. There have even been years when German wines were not harvested until November.

Italy is one of the largest producers of wine in the world, and also probably the greatest consumer. Unlike France and Germany, which have their respective wine districts, Italy has vineyards that extend from one end of the country to another; there is no province, village, or farm without its wines, for the climate is such that grapes can be grown anywhere in that sunny country. Because the weather is fairly consistent (unlike that of France and Germany), the wine crop never fails completely, but great vintages or great wines are unlikely. Italian white wines are pleasant to drink, and almost everyone likes them, but they cannot begin to compare with the finest products of France and Germany. Some of the best white wines of Italy are (not in any order of merit) Soave, white Chianti, Verdicchio, Frascati, Orvieto, and Capri.

The red wines are far better; most of them are what is called "drinkable," meaning they need not be slowly sipped, but can be drunk in gulps. Most Italian red wines lack the finesse of their French equivalent, but the average Italian does not fuss with wines the way a Frenchman does; the wines are there to drink and enjoy — and forget about vintages, and balance, and all of that nonsense. The most interesting red wines include Barolo, Barbaresco, Barbera, Gattinara, Grignolino, Sassella, Bardolino, Valpolicella, and, of course, Chianti. A word about this extremely popular wine: ordinary Chianti comes to the market in a straw-covered *fiasco*, which is necessary because the bottle has a rounded bottom and could not otherwise be placed upon the table. There is also an aged type called Chianti Classico, which reaches the market in regular bottles, and is far better.

Spain produces both red and white table wines, none of which are great, but are pleasant to drink. The two leading types are Rioja and Valdepenas. Nearby, in Portugal, a whole group of table wines are produced, including red, white and, *rosé* (pink). Some of the better-known Portuguese wines include Colares, Dao, and Grandjo. An interesting novelty is made in this country, *vinho verde*, green wine, a term that refers to the youth of the wine, not to its color. They are low in alcohol, slightly sparkling, and have a pleasant bouquet; the whites are far better than the reds.

The Swiss produce some light, rather unimportant table wines, but they do not travel well because of their low alcoholic content, and tend to lose their taste when they reach the United States. Although wine is produced all over Switzerland, the best comes from three regions — Vaud, Valais, and Neuchâtel.

North Africa has a great deal of wine production in Algeria, Morocco, and Tunis. Many of these wines are shipped to France in bulk, so that their comparatively high alcoholic strength may be blended with weak Gallic products in poor years. In South Africa the vineyards extend some 160 miles to the east of Cape Town. The white wines of South Africa are undistinguished; the reds are far more interesting.

Almost all the countries of South America (except Colombia and Venezuela) engage in some form of wine production, but Argentina and Chile are foremost in this field. In Argentina, much of the better wine is produced around Mendoza; almost all types of European wines are imitated here, some with more success than others. Probably the best wines of South America are made in Chile; although Argentina actually produces three times as much, Chile's product is generally superior.

The situation in the United States is very complex. Because of the size of the country, almost any climatic condition may be duplicated, and yet the average product that reaches the market is none too good. If it is good, it tends to be quite expensive. However, most of the ordinary wine shipped to the market is pasteurized, because the vintners are under the impression that Americans do not want to see any sediment develop in the bottle. In doing so, they also destroy the life of the wine, and minimize its taste. California ships wine to the market under two different classifications: the first includes imitations of European wines (like Burgundy or Bordeaux); the second type (usually unpasteurized) is based upon the type of grape used (Riesling or Sauvignon, for example). The most successful California wines are undoubtedly the "grape varietal" types, and the hope for the future of American wines lies in developing these wines, and not in unsuccessfully imitating European wines. Among the best types of red "varietals" are Cabernet-Sauvignon and Pinot Noir; the better white wines are made with Pinot Blanc, Pinot Chardonnay, Semillon Riesling, and Sauvignon Blanc. Recently vintners have been producing limited quantities of premium wines. If you can locate some of these you may find them quite enjoyable.

In New York State, most of the wines come from the northern part of the state, the Finger Lake district. European vines do not grow successfully there, so native vines such as Catawba, Elvira and Delaware are used. Very few red or *rosé* wines are produced, the vintners concentrating on white wines, champagnes and sherries which are good.

YOUR OWN WINE CELLAR

Nothing is pleasanter for wine enjoyment than devoting a small place in your home to wines. Of course, it is always possible to buy a bottle of wine as required, but wines are better when allowed a few days of rest, so that they may settle. Of course, a cellar in a private house is an ideal place for this, but it is not essential. Any cool dark place, free from drafts, away from cooking odors, and without extremes of heat and cold (no steam pipes, air-conditioning, etc.) will do. It may be a closet or any other spare space. The ideal temperature is 55°, but slightly higher or lower is permissible if there are no wide fluctuations. If there is danger of extreme cold or heat, the storage space should be lined with insulating material, which can be purchased at almost any hardware store. The wine bottles must, of course, be stored on their sides, so that the wine is actually in contact with the corks; otherwise the corks will dry out and the wine spoil. Good department stores sell wine racks made of wood or metal, with compartments for each individual bottle, should you wish to spend the money for this pleasant luxury.

Many wines are now available in half bottles; this is an ideal way of tasting, and of essaying your likes and dislikes at comparatively moderate cost. Some wine and liquor stores will allow you to buy a case of assorted half bottles (at cash prices), and this practise can be recommended to those who have a high degree of curiosity about the relative tastes and flavors of different wines. After sampling a large group, it should be fairly easy in the future to select several favorites.

Another good way to begin is by purchasing a small basic wine cellar, consisting of, say, a half-dozen or more bottles, and costing about $20 to $25. Naturally, any such list would be a matter of personal choice, but the following should act as a guide.

Red Wines:

1 Bordeaux (Gruard-Larose, Pontet-Canet, Leoville-Poy-ferre)
1 Burgundy (Volnay, Nuits-St. Georges, Chambertin)
1 Italian (Chianti, Valpolicella, Bardolino)
1 American (Pinot Noir, Cabernet-Sauvignon)

White Wines:

1 French (Pouilly-Fuisse, Pouilly-Fume)
1 Italian (Verdicchio, Orvieto, Soave)
1 German (Piesporter, Johannisberger)
1 American (Pinot Blanc, Sauvignon Blanc)

Now, what about wine in cooking? As previously mentioned, wines enhance the flavor of foods, bringing out unrealized subtleties of taste. For thousands of years, wine has been used as a cooking ingredient all over Europe, and the quality of European culinary art is well recognized the world over. In cookery, all of the rules about white wines with fish and red wines with meat, and about not using sweet wines, may be disregarded, because the cooking process changes all of that. Thus, many recipes in this book call for a white wine to be used with meat, or a red wine with a fish dish; exceptions for these cooking procedures do not cancel out or nullify what has been previously stated about drinking wines. Furthermore, no mother need feel the slightest qualms about feeding her children any dish made with wine; if the dish is cooked, the heat will evaporate all of the alcohol in the wine, making it perfectly suitable for serving even very young children.

As we go through life, we find that few pleasures remain as consistently rewarding as good food and good wine. Each alone is very worthwhile; the two together are often superb.

Myra Waldo

Appetizers

SHRIMP SOUFFLÉ

1 cup water	3 tablespoons flour
1 cup dry white wine	½ cup heavy cream
2 teaspoons salt	½ teaspoon dry mustard
1 onion	⅛ teaspoon cayenne pepper
1 pound raw shrimp, shelled and deveined	4 egg yolks
	4 egg whites
3 tablespoons butter	

Combine the water, ½ cup wine, 1 teaspoon salt, and the onion in a saucepan; bring to a boil. Add the shrimp, reduce heat, and cook over low heat 5 minutes. Drain. Strain the stock, reserving ¼ cup. Chop shrimp coarsely.

Melt the butter in a saucepan and stir in the flour. Gradually mix in the reserved stock, the remaining wine, and the cream, stirring steadily to the boiling point. Blend in the mustard, remaining salt, and the cayenne pepper; cook over low heat 5 minutes. Beat the egg yolks in a bowl; gradually mix in the hot sauce, stirring constantly to prevent curdling. Stir in the shrimp. Cool 10 minutes.

Beat the egg whites until stiff but not dry; fold into the shrimp mixture gently. Turn into a buttered 1½-quart soufflé dish; bake in a preheated 375° oven 35 minutes, or until browned and set. Serve immediately.

Serves 4-6.

Serve with a dry white Burgundy, a dry white German wine, or a Loire Valley wine like Pouilly-Fumé.

SPICED SHRIMP

2 cups water	2 bay leaves
2 cups dry white wine	2 cloves garlic, minced
2 teaspoons salt	1 cup chopped celery
¼ teaspoon Tabasco	and leaves
2 cloves	6 sprigs parsley
3 allspice	2 pounds raw shrimp,
6 peppercorns	shelled and deveined

Combine and bring to a boil all the ingredients but the shrimp. Add the shrimp, bring to a boil again, and cook over low heat 6 minutes. Cool the shrimp in the liquid, then chill at least 4 hours. Drain thoroughly. Pierce shrimp with cocktail picks or toothpicks for hors d'oeuvres, or serve as a first course.

Serves 6-8 as a first course.

Serve with a Loire wine like Pouilly-Fumé, a dry German white wine, or a white Burgundy.

SHRIMP COCKTAIL WITH SHERRY SAUCE

1 pound cooked shrimp, cleaned	½ cup chili sauce
	¼ cup dry sherry
1 cup diced cucumbers	1 teaspoon prepared
¼ cup mayonnaise	horseradish

Dice the shrimp and toss with the cucumbers. Mix together the mayonnaise, chili sauce, sherry, and horseradish. Toss with the shrimp. Chill 1 hour before serving.

Serves 4-6.

Serve with a dry German white wine, a Loire Valley wine like Pouilly-Fumé or Vouvray; or if you wish, with a *rosé*.

SHRIMP IN PAPERS

¼ pound Roquefort cheese	green olives
½ pound cream cheese	1½ pounds uncooked shrimp,
¾ cup dry white wine	shelled and deveined
½ cup chopped stuffed	6 slices lemon

Cream the Roquefort cheese and cream cheese until smooth; add the wine gradually, then the olives.

Cut 6 pieces of parchment paper or aluminum foil about 12 inches square; divide the cheese mixture among them and cover with several shrimp and a lemon slice. Bring two edges of the paper together and fold twice. Bring up other sides, and twist to make a secure closing. Bake in a 400° oven 30 minutes. Serve in the papers.

Serves 6.

Note: Smaller versions make excellent hot hors d'oeuvres.

Serve with a dry German white wine, a white Burgundy, or any dry Italian white wine like Verdicchio.

SCALLOPS LUTETIA

1½ pounds scallops	dry white wine
6 tablespoons butter	1 teaspoon salt
1½ cups sliced mushrooms	¼ teaspoon white pepper
1 cup heavy cream	3 egg yolks
2 cups champagne, or	

Wash and dry the scallops. If sea scallops are used, cut in half crosswise. Leave bay scallops whole.

Melt 3 tablespoons of the butter in a deep skillet; sauté the scallops for 3 minutes. Add the mushrooms, cream, wine, salt, and pepper. Cook over medium heat for 5 minutes. Remove the scallops and keep them warm. Cook the sauce over high heat until reduced to half.

Beat the egg yolks in a bowl. Gradually add the sauce, beating constantly to prevent curdling. Return the mixture to skillet with the scallops and the remaining butter. Reheat, but do not allow to boil. Taste for seasoning.

Serves 6-8.

Serve with champagne, a dry white Burgundy, or a dry German white wine.

CRABMEAT LUCULLUS

2 pounds crab meat	1½ teaspoons salt
4 tablespoons butter	Dash cayenne pepper
4 tablespoons flour	¾ cup dry white wine
2 cups light cream	

Pick over the crab meat, discarding any cartilage.

Melt the butter in a saucepan. Blend in the flour until smooth. Add the cream, stirring constantly to the boiling point. Mix in the salt, cayenne, pepper, wine. Fold in the crab meat. Taste for seasoning.

Pour the mixture into a buttered 1½-quart casserole. or into individual ovenproof dishes. Bake in a 400° oven 15 minutes.

Serves 6-8.

Serve with a dry German white wine, a white Burgundy, or an Alsatian wine.

GRATIN D'HOMARD
LOBSTER AU GRATIN

4 1¼-pound lobsters or	1 teaspoon salt
8 African lobster tails	⅛ teaspoon white pepper
¼ pound (1 stick) butter	1 cup heavy cream
¼ pound mushrooms, sliced	½ cup grated Gruyère or
¾ cup dry white wine	Swiss cheese
2 tablespoons flour	

Cook the lobster or tails in boiling salted water for 15 minutes. Drain and cool. Remove lobster meat; slice bodies and dice claws; or slice tail.

Melt 6 tablespoons butter in a skillet; sauté the lobster 5 minutes. Add the mushrooms, and sauté 2 minutes. Mix in the wine; cover, and cook over low heat 5 minutes. Mix the flour, salt, and pepper with the cream; add to the lobster, stirring constantly to the boiling point. Turn into a shallow baking dish or individual dishes. Sprinkle with cheese and dot with remaining butter. Bake in a 425° oven 10 minutes, or until delicately browned.

Serves 4-8.

Serve with a white Burgundy, champagne, a Loire Valley wine like Pouilly-Fumé, or a dry white Bordeaux.

OYSTERS WITH SEAFOOD SAUCE

½ pound raw shrimp,   ⅛ teaspoon cinnamon
   shelled and deveined   36 oysters on the half-shell
¼ pound crab meat   ½ cup grated Parmesan
½ cup dry white wine   cheese
1 cup chili sauce

Chop the shrimp very fine; combine in a saucepan with the crab meat, wine, chili sauce, and cinnamon. Cover, and cook over low heat 20 minutes. Taste for seasoning.

Arrange the oysters on a baking pan, and spoon the sauce over them. Sprinkle with the cheese. Bake in a 475° oven until cheese browns.

Serves 6-8.

BAKED OYSTERS AND CRAB MEAT

24 oysters on the half-shell   ¾ teaspoon salt
1 cup dry white wine   Dash cayenne pepper
6 tablespoons butter   ½ pound crab meat, flaked
2 tablespoons flour   4 tablespoons dry bread
½ cup heavy cream   crumbs

Remove the oysters from the shells. Scrub and dry the shells.

Bring the wine to a boil; add the oysters and cook over low heat 1 minute. Drain the oysters and strain the wine.

Melt 4 tablespoons of the butter in a saucepan; blend in the flour. Add the wine and cream, stirring steadily to the boiling point. Stir in the salt and cayenne pepper; cook over low heat 5 minutes. Mix the crab meat with ½ cup of the sauce; taste for seasoning. Divide the mixture among the shells and place an oyster over each. Cover with the remaining sauce, sprinkle with the bread crumbs, and dot with the remaining butter. Arrange on a baking sheet, and bake in a 475° oven 5 minutes. Serve immediately.

Serves 4-6.

Serve with a white Burgundy, an Alsatian wine like Traminer, or a dry German white wine.

ESCARGOTS À LA BOURGUIGNONNE
SNAILS IN GARLIC BUTTER

36 snails	1 teaspoon salt
1/3 pound butter	¼ teaspoon freshly ground
4 tablespoons finely chopped	black pepper
shallots or onion	¾ cup dry white wine
1 tablespoon minced garlic	¼ cup dry bread crumbs
3 tablespoons minced parsley	

If fresh snails are not available, buy canned snails, which come with shells separate.

Cream the butter and blend with the shallots, garlic, parsley, salt, and pepper. Place a little of the mixture in each shell and press a snail into it. Fill shells with remaining butter, packing in firmly. Arrange, filled side up, in 6 snail pans or a baking dish. Pour a little wine over them and sprinkle with bread crumbs. Bake in a 425° oven 10 minutes.

Serves 6.

Serve with a dry German white wine, champagne, or a Loire Valley wine like Pouilly-Fumé.

HERENGS MARINÉS
MARINATED HERRING

6 fresh herring	2 bay leaves
4 cups thinly sliced onions	2 cups dry white wine
2 tablespoons pickling spice	1 cup white wine vinegar
1 tablespoon salt	1/3 cup salad oil

Split the herring and discard the heads and bones; cut herring in half crosswise. In a heatproof glass or earthenware skillet or casserole, spread a layer of onion slices on the bottom, with half the pickling spice, salt, and 1 bay leaf over them. Arrange alternate layers of herring and onion slices over this, ending with the onion slices and remaining pickling spice, salt, and other bay leaf. Add the wine and vinegar; cover, and cook over low heat 25 minutes. Cool, and pour the oil over the top. Re-cover and refrigerate 48 hours before serving. Keeps 4-6 weeks.

Serves 12-18.

Note: If fresh herring is not available, then use salt

herring. Soak in cold water 24 hours, changing the water a few times. Decrease salt in recipe to 1 teaspoon.

BOULETTES DE FROMAGE
CHEESE BALLS

8 ounces Camembert or Brie cheese	softened
1 cup dry white wine	1 cup ground blanched almonds
½ pound (2 sticks) butter,	Toasted blanched almonds

Carefully remove the rind of the cheese. Marinate the trimmed cheese in the wine 8 hours, turning it several times. Drain. Force the cheese through a food mill, or mash smooth. Beat in the butter. Chill 3 hours. Form teaspoons of the mixture into balls. Chill again, then roll in the ground almonds. Place a whole almond in each ball.

Makes about 60.

Serve with a dry red Bordeaux or Burgundy, or a dry Italian red wine like Bardolino.

DELICES D'EMMENTHAL
FRIED CHEESE STICKS

4 tablespoons butter	Swiss cheese
1 1/3 cups sifted flour	3 egg yolks, beaten
½ cup dry white wine	1 egg
1 cup milk	¼ cup light cream
¾ teaspoon salt	1 tablespoon olive oil
Dash cayenne pepper	¾ cup dry bread crumbs
2 cups (½ pound) grated	1 cup vegetable oil

Melt the butter in a saucepan; blend in 1/3 cup of the flour. Gradually add the wine and milk, stirring steadily to the boiling point. Stir in the salt and cayenne pepper; cook over low heat 10 minutes, stirring frequently. Remove from heat, and mix in the cheese until melted. Beat in the egg yolks.

Turn into a buttered oblong dish to a depth of 1 inch. Cover with foil or waxed paper and chill. Cut into strips about 3 inches long and ½ inch wide. Beat the whole egg with the cream and olive oil. Dip the sticks in the remaining flour, then in the egg mixture, and finally in the bread crumbs, coating them thoroughly.

Heat the vegetable oil in a skillet until it bubbles. Fry the sticks in it until browned on all sides. Drain. Don't crowd the pan, and keep oil very hot, or the sticks will melt.

Makes about 24.

Serve with an Alsatian wine like Riesling, a dry German white wine, or a dry red Bordeaux or Burgundy.

AUBERGINES À LA GRECQUE
EGGPLANT IN OIL

1 medium eggplant	¼ teaspoon thyme
2 teaspoons salt	4 peppercorns, crushed
½ cup olive oil	2 coriander seeds
¾ cup dry white wine	1½ cups peeled, chopped
1 bay leaf	tomatoes

Peel the eggplant, and cut as for french fried potatoes. Sprinkle with the salt, and let stand 30 minutes. Drain very well.

Heat the oil in a skillet; lightly brown the eggplant in it. Remove the eggplant. To the oil remaining in the skillet, add the wine, bay leaf, thyme, peppercorns, coriander seeds, and tomatoes. Bring to a boil, and cook over low heat 15 minutes. Return the eggplant to skillet. Cook over low heat 15 minutes. Taste for seasoning. Serve cold.

Serves 4.

ARTICHOKES À LA GRECQUE

1 package frozen artichoke hearts	½ cup dry white wine
12 very small white onions	1½ teaspoons salt
1 clove garlic, minced	¼ teaspoon freshly ground black pepper
¼ cup olive oil	¼ cup water
3 tablespoons lemon juice	

Let the artichoke hearts thaw sufficiently to separate. In a saucepan, combine the remaining ingredients. Bring to a boil, and cook over low heat 25 minutes. Add the artichoke hearts. Cook 5 minutes. Taste for seasoning. Pour into a glass or pottery dish. Cool, then refrigerate until needed. Will keep about 2 weeks.

Serves 3-4.

CAPPELLI DI FUNGHI RIPIENI
STUFFED MUSHROOM CAPS

2 pounds firm white mushrooms	½ cup dry white wine
	1 teaspoon salt
4 tablespoons olive oil	¼ teaspoon freshly ground
4 tablespoons butter	black pepper
1 clove garlic, minced	1 egg yolk, beaten
1 tablespoon flour	½ cup dry bread crumbs

Wash and dry the mushrooms; remove the stems and chop them. Heat 1 tablespoon oil and 1 tablespoon butter in a skillet; sauté the mushrooms and garlic 2 minutes. Blend in the flour, and add the wine, salt, and pepper. Cook over medium heat 5 minutes, or until liquid is evaporated, stirring frequently. Cool 10 minutes, then mix in the egg yolk. Stuff the mushroom caps.

Pour the remaining oil into a shallow baking dish; arrange the mushrooms in it. Sprinkle with the bread crumbs and dot with the remaining butter. Bake in a 375° oven 15 minutes. Serve hot or cold.

Serves 4-6.

Serve with champagne, or a *rosé* wine.

OEUFS À LA BOURGUIGNONNE
EGGS IN WINE

10 slices bacon, diced	black pepper
3 tablespoons butter	1 cup beef broth
½ cup chopped onion	1 cup dry red wine
1 clove garlic, minced	1 bay leaf
2 tablespoons flour	⅛ teaspoon thyme
1¼ teaspoons salt	2 tablespoons minced parsley
¼ teaspoon freshly ground	8 eggs

Fry the bacon until crisp. Drain. Melt the butter in a saucepan; sauté the onion and garlic until lightly browned. Blend in the flour, salt, and pepper, then gradually add the broth and wine, stirring steadily to the boiling point. Add the bay leaf, thyme, and parsley; cook over low heat 20 minutes. Strain into a skillet. Bring to a boil again and carefully poach the eggs in it, no more than 2 at a time. Serve on sautéed or toasted French bread, with the sauce over them, and the bacon sprinkled on top.

Serves 4-8.

Serve with a dry red Bordeaux or Burgundy, including a Beaujolais, a dry Italian red wine like Bardolino.

UOVA ALLA CACCIATORA
EGGS, HUNTER'S STYLE

¼ pound chicken livers
4 tablespoons olive oil
¼ cup chopped onion
1¼ teaspoons salt
¼ teaspoon freshly ground black pepper
¼ teaspoon basil

¼ cup peeled, chopped tomatoes
¼ cup dry white wine
4 eggs
4 slices buttered toast
1 tablespoon parsley

Wash the livers, cut away any discolored spots. Cut in half.

Heat the oil in a skillet; sauté the chopped onions 5 minutes. Add the livers; sauté 5 minutes, mixing occasionally. Stir in the salt, pepper, basil, tomatoes, and wine. Bring to a boil, and cook over low heat 5 minutes. Carefully break the eggs into the pan, cover, and cook until set, about 3 minutes. Transfer each egg to a piece of toast and cover with the sauce. Sprinkle with the parsley.

Serves 2-4.

Serve with a dry red Bordeaux or Burgundy, or a dry Italian red wine like Barbera.

EGGS AMANDINE

4 tablespoons butter	6 eggs
2 tablespoons grated onion	½ cup heavy cream
½ cup ground almonds	1 teaspoon salt
¼ cup boiled ham, ground	¼ teaspoon freshly ground
½ cup champagne or	black pepper
dry white wine	

Melt the butter in a skillet. Add the grated onion, almonds, and ham. Sauté for 5 minutes, stirring almost constantly. Add the champagne or white wine. Cook over low heat for 3 minutes.

Beat together the eggs, cream, salt, and pepper in a bowl. Pour over the almond mixture, and cook to desired consistency, stirring constantly. Do not overcook. Serve in patty shells or on toast squares.

Serves 4-6.

Serve with a light red Bordeaux, Burgundy, or a dry Italian red wine like Valpolicella.

MOUSSE DE FOIE DE VOLAILLE
CHICKEN LIVER MOUSSE

1 pound chicken livers	¼ cup heavy cream
⅜ pound (1½ sticks) butter	¾ teaspoon salt
¼ cup chopped onion	¼ teaspoon freshly ground
½ cup Madeira or	black pepper
sweet sherry	

Wash the livers, remove any discolored spots, and dry. Cut the livers in small pieces.

Melt 4 tablespoons butter in a skillet; sauté the livers and onion 5 minutes. Empty into a blender bowl or onto a board. Add the wine to the skillet; cook over high heat 5 minutes. Add to the livers. Purée in the blender, gradually adding the cream, salt, and pepper until a smooth paste is formed. Or chop very fine, gradually adding the cream and the seasoning, and force the mixture through a fine sieve. Taste for seasoning, and pack into a bowl or crock. Cover, and chill 4 hours. Serve in the crock, or unmold and serve with slices of French bread.

Makes about 2 cups.
Serve with a *rosé* wine.

KÄSEBRÖTCHEN
WINE-CHEESE TOAST

6 slices stale bread	¾ cup freshly grated
1 cup dry white wine	Parmesan cheese
2 eggs, beaten	3 tablespoons butter

Trim the crusts off the bread. Dip the slices one at a time in the wine. Beat the eggs and mix in the cheese. Dip the slices in the mixture, coating them well. Arrange on a well-buttered baking sheet and dot with the butter. Bake in a 375° oven 15 minutes, or until bread is browned, turning the slices once. Serve hot.

Serves 6.

Serve with a white Swiss wine like Fendant, a dry German white wine, or an Alsatian wine like Traminer.

SWISS FONDUE

1 clove garlic	⅛ teaspoon white pepper
2¼ cups dry white wine	⅛ teaspoon nutmeg
1 pound Gruyère or	3 tablespoons kirsch
Swiss cheese, grated	(cherry liqueur)
1½ tablespoons potato flour	French bread cubes
½ teaspoon salt	

A chafing dish is customarily used for making fondue. If you do not have one, use the bottom of a double boiler to hold the water, and an earthenware bowl for the fondue. Have enough hot water in the bottom part of the chafing dish or double boiler to barely touch the bowl. Light the burner of the chafing dish, or place double boiler over low heat.

Rub the chafing dish or bowl with the garlic and add 2 cups wine; place over the water. Heat the wine, then stir in the cheese until melted. Mix the potato flour with the remaining wine and add to the cheese mixture, stirring steadily. Let cook 3 minutes. Blend in the salt, pepper, nutmeg, and kirsch. Provide a fork for each guest with which to spear the cubes of French bread — the bread cubes should then be dipped in the fondue.

Serves 4-6.

Serve with a white Swiss wine like Neuchâtel or Fendant, or an Alsatian wine like Traminer, or a dry German white wine.

Soup

CIORBA DE CEAPA
RUMANIAN ONION SOUP

3 tablespoons butter
3 cups diced onion
2 teaspoons sugar
5 cups beef broth
1 cup diced potatoes
¼ teaspoon celery seed
1 cup dry white wine

2 tablespoons lemon juice
1 teaspoon sugar
¼ teaspoon freshly ground
   black pepper
1 cup heavy cream
2 tablespoons minced parsley

Melt the butter in a saucepan; sauté the onions and sugar until browned. Add the broth, potato, and celery seed. Cover, bring to a boil, and cook over low heat 30 minutes. Purée in a blender, or force through a food mill.

Return to the saucepan and stir in the wine, lemon juice, sugar, and pepper. Bring to a boil, and cook over low heat 10 minutes. Gradually blend in the cream; heat, but do not let boil. Taste for seasoning, sprinkle with the parsley, and serve.

Serves 6-8.

CREAMED ONION SOUP

4 tablespoons butter
4 cups thinly sliced onion
1½ tablespoons flour
4 cups chicken broth
2 cups dry white wine
1 teaspoon salt

¼ teaspoon white pepper
2 egg yolks
1 cup heavy cream
Grated Gruyère or
   Swiss cheese

Melt the butter in a saucepan; sauté the sliced onions over low heat until browned. Blend in the flour. Add the broth, wine, salt, and pepper, mixing steadily to the boiling point. Cover loosely, and cook over low heat 25 minutes.

Beat the egg yolks and cream in a bowl. Gradually add some of the hot soup, stirring steadily to prevent curdling. Return to balance of soup. Taste for seasoning. Heat, stirring steadily, but do not let boil. Serve with a bowl of grated cheese.

Serves 6-8.

CREAM OF MUSHROOM SOUP

½ cup dried mushrooms	2 cups milk
½ cup water	1¼ teaspoons salt
1 pound fresh mushrooms	¼ teaspoon freshly ground
¼ pound butter	black pepper
2 tablespoons flour	¼ cup dry sherry
2 cups heavy cream	Minced parsley

Soak the dried mushrooms in the water for 2 hours. Drain, reserving the water, and chop.

Chop the stems of the fresh mushrooms. Melt the butter in a skillet. Sauté the fresh chopped mushrooms 5 minutes. Add the mushroom caps and cook 5 minutes. Remove the mushroom caps. Blend the flour into butter and mushroom stems mixture. Gradually add the cream and milk, stirring constantly until thickened, then add the salt and pepper. Add the dried mushrooms and the water. Cook 20 minutes.

Just before serving, add the sherry and the mushroom caps. Serve sprinkled with the parsley.

Serves 6.

· WATERZOOI DE POULET
BELGIAN CHICKEN-IN-THE-POT

2 2-pound broilers, quartered	1 tablespoon salt
2 veal knuckles	½ teaspoon white pepper
6 cups water	3 slices lemon
2 stalks celery	2 cups dry white wine
1 parsnip	3 tablespoons butter
4 sprigs parsley	½ cup dry bread crumbs

Wash and dry the chicken and giblets. Combine the gizzards, livers, veal knuckles, water, celery, parsnips, parsley, salt, pepper, and lemon in a saucepan. Bring to a boil; cover, and cook over low heat 2 hours. Strain.

Combine the stock, wine, and butter in a casserole. Bring to a boil and add the chicken; cover, and cook over low heat 30 minutes, or until chicken is tender. Stir in the bread crumbs, taste for seasoning, and serve directly from the casserole in deep bowls.

Serves 4-8.

OXTAIL SOUP

1 oxtail	1½ cups dry red wine
¼ cup flour	6 cups water
3 tablespoons butter	2 teaspoons salt
½ pound ground beef	½ teaspoon freshly ground
1 cup chopped onion	black pepper
½ cup chopped celery	2 teaspoons paprika
1 tomato, peeled and	1 bay leaf
chopped	½ cup diced potatoes

Have the oxtail cut into 2-inch pieces. Wash, cover with water, and bring to a boil. Drain and dry. Roll in the flour.

Melt the butter in a saucepan; add the oxtail pieces, and cook until brown. Add the beef, onion, and celery, and continue browning. Mix in the tomato, wine, the 6 cups water, salt, pepper, paprika, bay leaf, and potato. Bring to a boil, cover, and cook over low heat 3 hours. Remove the oxtail pieces. Cut the meat from the bone into small pieces. Reserve. Discard the bones and bay leaf. Purée the soup in a blender, or force through a sieve. Return to saucepan, add the reserved meat, heat, and serve.

Serves 6-8.

WEINSUPPE
GERMAN WINE SOUP

3 egg whites	⅛ teaspoon ground cloves
½ teaspoon salt	1 teaspoon sugar
4 cups dry white wine	3 egg yolks
¼ teaspoon cinnamon	

Beat the egg whites and salt until stiff. Drop by the heaping teaspoon into boiling water. Cook over low heat 5 minutes. Remove carefully with a slotted spoon.

While the egg whites are cooking, bring the wine, cinnamon, cloves, and sugar to a boil. Beat the egg yolks in a bowl; gradually add a little of the hot wine mixture, stirring steadily to prevent curdling. Return to the balance of the wine mixture. Heat, but do not let boil.

Serve the soup with the egg-white dumplings afloat. Serves 4-6.

TOMATO WINE SOUP

1 cup dry white wine	1 teaspoon sugar
3 cups beef broth	¼ teaspoon freshly ground
4 cups tomato juice	black pepper
½ cup sliced onion	2 cloves
2 sprigs parsley	¼ cup dry sherry
2 stalks celery	

Combine the wine, broth, tomato juice, onion slices, parsley, celery, sugar, pepper, and cloves in a saucepan. Bring to a boil, and cook over low heat 20 minutes. Strain, return to saucepan, and mix in the sherry. Taste for seasoning. Heat and serve in bouillon cups, with a slice of lemon sprinkled with paprika in each.

Serves 8-10.

BISQUE DE HOMARD
LOBSTER BISQUE

1½-pound live lobster	¼ teaspoon thyme
6 tablespoons butter	4 tablespoons flour
¼ cup chopped onion	5 cups chicken broth
¼ cup grated carrot	2 teaspoons salt
¼ cup cognac	Dash cayenne pepper
¾ cup dry sherry	1½ cups heavy cream
1 cup bottled clam juice	

Have the lobster cut into 4 sections, shells and all, and the claws cracked. Melt half the butter in a saucepan; sauté the onion and carrot 5 minutes. Add the lobster; sauté 5 minutes, or until lobster turns red. Warm the cognac, pour over the lobster, and set aflame. When flames die, stir in the sherry, clam juice, and thyme. Cover, and cook over low heat 15 minutes. Remove the lobster pieces; reserve the sauce. Scoop the lobster meat out of the shells and chop coarsely. Break up the lobster shells and pulverize in a blender with 2 tablespoons sauce, or put through a food chopper.

Melt the remaining butter in a saucepan; blend in the flour. Gradually add the chicken broth, stirring steadily to the boiling point. Add the salt, cayenne, reserved sauce, and pulverized shells. Cover, and cook over low heat 1 hour. Strain. Stir in the cream and lobster meat. Heat, and taste for seasoning.

Serves 6-8.

SHRIMP-MUSHROOM BISQUE

4 tablespoons butter	2 cups dry white wine
2 pounds raw shrimp, shelled, deveined, and diced	1 stalk celery
	1/8 teaspoon cayenne pepper
	1/8 teaspoon nutmeg
3/4 cup chopped mushrooms	1 cup heavy cream
2 cups bottled clam juice	

Melt the butter in a saucepan; sauté the shrimp and mushrooms 5 minutes. Mix in the clam juice and wine. Add the celery, cayenne pepper, and nutmeg. Cook over low heat 20 minutes. Discard the celery, and purée the soup in a blender, or force through a food mill. Return to saucepan. Stir in the cream and season to taste. Heat, but do not let boil.

Serves 6-8.

SOPA DE PESCADO
SHRIMP AND SCALLOP SOUP

6 tablespoons butter	shelled and deveined
1 cup finely chopped onion	1 pound scallops
4 cups bottled clam juice	1/8 teaspoon dried ground chili peppers
4 cups dry white wine	
1/2 teaspoon white pepper	1/2 cup ground almonds
1 cup diced white bread	1 cup heavy cream
1 cup milk	1/2 teaspoon paprika
1 pound raw shrimp,	2 hard-cooked eggs, chopped

Melt the butter in a saucepan; sauté the chopped onion until soft and lightly browned. Mix in the clam juice, wine, and pepper; bring to a boil, and cook over low heat 30 minutes. Soak the bread in the milk and mash smooth; add to soup in the saucepan and cook over low heat 10 minutes. Pour boiling water over the shrimp; drain. Add to the soup, with the scallops and chili peppers. Cook 5 minutes. Blend in the almonds, cream, paprika, and eggs. Cook 5 minutes longer. Taste for seasoning.

Serves 8-10.

CIOPPINO
SAN FRANCISCO FISH SOUP

1½-pound live lobster
24 small clams
2 pounds red snapper, sea bass, etc.
1 pound raw shrimp, shelled and deveined
¾ cup olive oil
1½ cups chopped onion
1 cup diced green peppers

3 cloves garlic, minced
1 29-ounce can tomatoes
2 8-ounce cans tomato sauce
2 teaspoons salt
¾ teaspoon freshly ground black pepper
1 bay leaf
2 cups dry red wine
½ teaspoon oregano

Have the lobster cut up in the shell, the bodies cut in half lengthwise, then in 3 pieces crosswise, and the claws in 2 pieces. Scrub the clams, and wash under cold running water for a few minutes. Cut the fish in bite-size pieces. Wash the shrimp. Keep all the fish refrigerated until needed.

Heat the oil in a heavy saucepan; sauté the chopped onions, green peppers, and garlic 10 minutes, stirring frequently. Add the tomatoes, tomato sauce, salt, and pepper. Cover and cook over low heat 2 hours, mixing frequently. Mix in the bay leaf, wine, and oregano; cook 10 minutes longer. Taste for seasoning.

Put all the fish and other seafood in a deep casserole; pour the sauce over it. Bring to a boil, cover, and cook over low heat 20 minutes. Serve in deep plates, with garlic toast.

Serves 6-8.

Serve with an Italian red wine.

ZUPPA DI PESCE
FISH SOUP, ITALIAN STYLE

3 pounds assorted sliced fish
1/3 cup olive oil
1½ teaspoon salt
½ teaspoon black pepper
1 teaspoon finely chopped
    bay leaf

1½ cups chopped onion
1 clove garlic, minced
2 tablespoons tomato paste
3 cups dry white wine
1 cup boiling water

Buy as many varieties of fish as possible, but be sure to include some eel. Cut the fish into serving-size pieces. Wash and dry.

Heat the oil in a heavy saucepan; brown the fish in it lightly. Season with the salt, pepper, and bay leaf; cook over low heat 15 minutes, turning the pieces once. Carefully remove the fish and keep warm. In the oil remaining in the pan, sauté the chopped onions 10 minutes. Mix in the garlic, tomato paste, and wine, then the boiling water. Cook over low heat 25 minutes. Return the fish to pan and cook 10 minutes longer. Taste for seasoning. Serve in deep plates with sautéed bread, rubbed with garlic. The resulting dish is a cross between a soup and a stew.

Serves 6-8.

BOUILLABAISSE MARSEILLAISE
FISH SOUP, MARSEILLE STYLE

1/3 cup olive oil
1½ cups chopped onion
2 cloves garlic, minced
2 cups chopped fresh
    tomatoes, or drained
    canned tomatoes
2 cups dry white wine
2 cups bottled clam juice
1 bay leaf
½ teaspoon thyme
⅛ teaspoon crushed fennel
    seeds

⅛ teaspoon saffron
2 pounds assorted fish, cut
    in serving-size pieces
1 lobster, cut up in the shell
¾ pound raw shrimp,
    shelled and deveined
½ pound scallops
12 mussels or clams, or both,
    scrubbed
2 tablespoons chopped
    parsley

Heat the oil in a large kettle; sauté the onion and garlic 5 minutes. Mix in the tomatoes, wine, clam juice, bay leaf, thyme, fennel, and saffron. Bring to a boil, and cook over low heat 30 minutes. Add the fish and other seafood. Cook 20 minutes longer. Taste for seasoning. Stir in the parsley. Serve in deep plates with garlic-rubbed toasted French bread.

Serves 6.

TOMATO-CLAM BROTH

4 tablespoons butter	2 cups dry white wine
1½ cups chopped onion	6 cups bottled clam juice
2 cups chopped tomatoes	¼ teaspoon white pepper
1 clove garlic, minced	2 tablespoons minced parsley

Melt the butter in a saucepan; sauté the chopped onion 10 minutes. Add the tomatoes and garlic; cook over low heat 5 minutes. Mix in the wine, clam juice, and pepper. Cook over medium-low heat 30 minutes. Stir in the parsley, taste for seasoning, and serve with sautéed bread slices.

Serves 6-8.

ZUPPA DI VONGOLE
CLAM SOUP, ITALIAN STYLE

48 small clams	½ cup canned tomatoes,
3 cups dry white wine	chopped
½ cup olive oil	2 stalks celery
¾ cup chopped onion	¼ teaspoon marjoram
2 cloves garlic, minced	2 tablespoons minced parsley

Scrub the clams and wash under cold running water; combine in a kettle with the wine. Cover, and cook over high heat until clams open. Drain, reserving the stock. Remove the clams from the shells.

Heat the oil in a saucepan; sauté the onion until lightly browned. Add the garlic, tomatoes, celery, marjoram, and reserved stock. Cook over high heat 10 minutes. Discard the celery, and add the clams and parsley. Cook 1 minute. Serve in deep soup plates with croutons.

Serves 4-6.

CREAM OF CLAM SOUP

2 10-ounce cans minced clams
¾ cup dry white wine
¼ teaspoon white pepper
2 tablespoons butter
2 egg yolks
½ cup heavy cream
1 tablespoon minced parsley

Combine the undrained clams, the wine, pepper, and butter in a saucepan. Bring to a boil, and cook over heat 3 minutes.

Beat the egg yolks and cream in a bowl; gradually add some of the hot soup, stirring steadily to prevent curdling. Return to balance of soup and heat, stirring steadily, but do not let boil. Taste for seasoning. Serve immediately, sprinkled with the parsley.

Serves 4-5.

MUSSEL CHOWDER

36 mussels
½ cup water
1 large carrot, chopped
1 large onion, chopped
1 heaping tablespoon chopped parsley
1 green pepper, chopped
1 tablespoon thyme
¾ cup white wine
1 bay leaf
1 clove garlic
Salt
Freshly ground black pepper

Clean and scrub the mussels. Place them in a pot and steam them open with the water. Drain, reserving the liquid.

In another saucepan, combine the carrot, onion, parsley, green pepper, thyme, white wine, bay leaf, garlic, and the reserved liquid. Cook over low heat 45 minutes.

Add the mussels and cook 20 minutes. Discard the garlic and bay leaf, and add salt and pepper to taste. Serve in deep plates.

Serves 4-6.

BILLI BI
CREAM OF MUSSEL SOUP

2 pounds mussels	black pepper
1 cup dry white wine	Dash cayenne pepper
2 shallots, sliced	2 tablespoons butter
2 onions, quartered	1 small bay leaf
2 sprigs parsley	½ teaspoon thyme
1 teaspoon salt	1 egg yolk
¼ teaspoon freshly ground	2 cups heavy cream

Scrub the mussels well and wash under cold running water until water runs clear. Combine in a large pan with the wine, shallots, onions, parsley, salt, pepper, cayenne, butter, bay leaf, and thyme. Cover, and bring to a boil. Cook until the mussels have opened. Discard any mussels that do not open. Remove the mussels and discard the shells.

Strain the liquid through a double thickness of cheese-cloth. Beat the egg yolk and cream; gradually add the mussel liquid, stirring steadily to prevent curdling.

Return to pan and cook, stirring steadily until thickened slightly, but do not let boil. Serve hot or ice-cold, garnished with the mussels.

Serves 4.

TOMATO-CRAB SOUP

6 tablespoons butter	3 cups diced cooked
1 cup chopped onion	tomatoes
4 tablespoons chopped celery	Salt
5 tablespoons flour	Pepper
1 quart milk	¾ pound crab meat, flaked
1 pint light cream	½ cup dry sherry

Melt the butter in a saucepan; sauté the onion and celery 10 minutes. Blend in the flour until smooth.

Gradually add the milk, stirring to the boiling point. Stir in the cream. Bring to a boil, and cook 5 minutes, stirring constantly. Purée the tomatoes in a blender, or force through a sieve. Add to the white sauce. Season with salt and pepper to taste. Add the crab meat and sherry; heat and serve.

Serves 8.

CREAM OF KING CRAB SOUP

1 pound king crab (in shell)
¾ cup diced onion
2 stalks celery, sliced
4 tablespoons butter
4 tablespoons flour
1½ quarts hot water

1 tablespoon salt
¼ teaspoon white pepper
¼ teaspoon thyme
1½ cups light cream
1½ cups dry white wine

If frozen crab is used, thaw it. Remove the meat and slice. Crush the shells. Sauté the shells, onion, and celery in the butter for 10 minutes. Blend in the flour; gradually add the water, salt, pepper, and thyme, stirring steadily to the boiling point. Cook over low heat 1½ hours. Strain. Add the cream, wine, and crab meat. Cook 10 minutes. Taste for seasoning.

Serves 8-10.

CHEESE SOUP

4 tablespoons butter
¼ cup finely chopped onion
½ cup grated carrot
¼ cup chopped celery
2 tablespoons flour
2 cups chicken broth
½ teaspoon salt

Dash cayenne pepper
½ cup dry sherry
2 cups (½ pound) grated Cheddar cheese
2 tablespoons chopped pimientos

Melt the butter in a saucepan; sauté the onion, carrot, and celery 10 minutes, stirring frequently, but do not let brown. Blend in the flour; gradually add the broth, stirring steadily to the boiling point. Stir in the salt and cayenne pepper. Cook over low heat 10 minutes. Stir in the sherry, and the cheese until melted. Serve sprinkled with the pimientos.

Serves 4.

OBSTSUPPE
FRUIT SOUP

1 pound plums
1 pound peaches
½ pound cherries
4 cups water
4 cups dry white wine
1 cup sugar

½ teaspoon cinnamon
1 tablespoon arrowroot or
  cornstarch
2 tablespoons sweet sherry
Whipped cream

Wash the fruit. Cut the plums and peaches in half, and discard the pits. Pit the cherries. Combine the fruits with the water, wine, sugar, and cinnamon. Bring to a boil, and cook over low heat 30 minutes, or until the fruits are very soft. Pureé in a blender, or force through a sieve. Return to the saucepan.

Mix the arrowroot with the sherry and stir into the soup. Cook over low heat, stirring steadily until thickened. Chill. Serve with a spoon of whipped cream in each plate.

Serves 6-8.

COLD RED RASPBERRY SOUP

1 cup boiling water
1 quart fresh raspberries
1 tablespoon cornstarch
2 tablespoons cold water

¼ cup sugar
1/3 cup orange juice
½ cup dry sherry

Add the boiling water to the berries; cover, and cook 10 minutes. Force berries through a sieve. Mix cornstarch with cold water. Add with the sugar to hot purée. Cook over low heat, stirring until mixture begins to thicken; cover, and cook over low heat 10 minutes. Cool slightly and mix in the orange juice. Chill. Add the sherry just before serving. Serve very cold, garnished with mint leaves.

Serves 4-6.

Fish

CACIUCCO
LEGHORN FISH STEW

3 pounds assorted salt-water
    fish
12 clams
½ cup olive oil
¾ cup chopped onion
2 cloves garlic, minced
1½ cups dry red wine

1 20-ounce can tomatoes,
    drained
1½ teaspoons salt
½ teaspoon crushed dried
    red peppers
2 tablespoons minced parsley

Be sure the fish you buy is salt-water fish, and consists of more than one kind, cut in slices. Wash and dry the fish. Scrub the clams under cold running water until water runs clear.

Heat the oil in a saucepan; sauté the onion and garlic 5 minutes. Add the wine; cook until reduced to half. Mix in the tomatoes, salt, and red peppers. Arrange the sliced fish in it. Bring to a boil, and cook over low heat 25 minutes. Add the clams and parsley; cover, and cook 5 minutes longer, or until clams open. Discard any clams that do not open. Serve in deep plates with garlic toast.

Serves 6-8.

Serve with a dry white Rhône wine like Hermitage Blanc or a Pouilly-Fuissé, or a *rosé*.

MATELOTE
FISH STEW IN WHITE WINE

3 pounds assorted fresh-water fish	¼ teaspoon freshly ground black pepper
1 slice bacon	1 bay leaf, finely crushed
3 tablespoons butter	¼ teaspoon marjoram
3 tablespoons olive oil	⅛ teaspoon nutmeg
3 tablespoons flour	2 tablespoons minced parsley
6 cups dry white wine	¼ cup cognac
1 clove garlic, minced	Sautéed French bread slices
2 teaspoons salt	

Buy a varied assortment of fish, and include eel if possible. Cut in serving-size pieces. Cover the bacon with water; bring to a boil, then drain and chop coarsely.

Heat the butter and oil in a casserole; brown the bacon in it. Stir in the flour until browned. Gradually add the wine, stirring constantly to the boiling point. Mix in the garlic, salt, pepper, bay leaf, marjoram, nutmeg, and parsley. Cover, and cook over low heat 30 minutes. Add the fish and cook 20 minutes. Heat the cognac, set it aflame, and pour it into the casserole; shake the casserole until flames die. Arrange sautéed bread slices on top around the edges of the casserole. Serve in deep plates.

Serves 6-8.

Serve with a white Burgundy like Chablis, a white Rhône wine like Hermitage Blanc, a dry Loire Valley wine like Sancerre, or a *rosé*.

LA POCHOUSE BOURGUIGNONNE
BURGUNDY FISH STEW

4 pounds mixed fresh-water fish, after trimming	2 cloves garlic, minced
¼ pound (1 stick) butter	1 teaspoon meat extract
2 tablespoons diced bacon	4 tablespoons flour
2 quarts dry white wine	2½ teaspoons salt
1 bay leaf ⎫ tied	½ teaspoon freshly ground pepper
6 sprigs parsley ⎬ together	½ cup cognac
½ teaspoon thyme	Sautéed French bread slices

Four or more types of fish are needed for this dish. Pike, trout, carp, white fish, and eel are good choices. Cut the fish into pieces 1½ inches thick. Melt 6 tablespoons butter in a deep saucepan, add the bacon, and sauté until browned. Add the wine, bay leaf and parsley, thyme, and garlic; bring to a boil. Cook over low heat 20 minutes. Add fish and cook over medium heat 20 minutes. Blend in the meat extract, and the flour kneaded with the remaining butter. Add salt and pepper; taste for seasoning. Set the cognac aflame and add, shaking pan till flames die down.

Put the sautéed bread slices (rubbed with garlic, if you like) in the bottom of a deep tureen, and pour the soup over it. Serve at once.

Serves 8-10.

CAZUELA DE MARISCOS
MIXED SEAFOOD CASSEROLE

¼ cup olive oil
1½ cups chopped onion
1 cup julienne-cut green
   peppers
1½ cups peeled, diced
   potatoes
2 teaspoons salt
½ teaspoon freshly ground
   black pepper
1 clove garlic, minced
2 teaspoons finely chopped
   bay leaves

1½ cups dry white wine
4 tablespoons tomato paste
1 cup boiling water
1 pound fillet of sole, cut in
   bite-size pieces
1 pound raw shrimp,
   shelled and deveined
½ pound crab meat
2 tablespoons minced parsley
Sautéed French or Italian
bread slices

Heat the oil in a casserole; sauté the onion 10 minutes. Add the green peppers and potatoes; cook 5 minutes. Mix in the salt, pepper, garlic, bay leaves, wine, tomato paste, and boiling water. Cover, and cook over low heat 20 minutes. Add the fillet of sole; cook 15 minutes. Mix in the shrimp and crab meat; cook 10 minutes. Taste for seasoning. Sprinkle with the parsley. Arrange sautéed bread around the edge of the casserole.

Serves 6-8.

Serve with a white Burgundy, a dry German white wine, a Loire Valley wine like Pouilly-Fumé, or a *rosé*.

CAZUELA DE PESCADO
FISH, POTATO, AND RICE CASSEROLE

½ cup raw long-grain rice
½ cup olive oil
2 cups thinly sliced onion
2 cups thinly sliced potatoes
2 pounds fillets of fish,
    cut in 2-inch pieces

2 teaspoons salt
¾ teaspoon freshly ground
    black pepper
1 cup diced tomatoes
1½ cups dry white wine
1 cup bottled clam juice

Wash the rice under cold running water until water runs clear. Grease a casserole with 2 tablespoons of the oil. Spread half the sliced onions on the bottom with half the sliced potatoes over them. Spread the fish over the potatoes; sprinkle with half the salt and pepper. Cover the fish with the remaining onions, then the remaining potatoes, the rice, and tomatoes. Sprinkle with the remaining salt and pepper. Add the wine and clam juice. Cover, and bake in a 350° oven 1 hour, removing the cover for the last 10 minutes.

Serves 6-8.

Serve with a white Burgundy, especially a Chablis, a Rhône wine like Hermitage Blanc, an Alsatian white wine like Sylvaner, or a *rosé*.

CASSEROLE DE POISSON
FISH CASSEROLE

4 slices bacon
6 fillets sole
2½ teaspoons salt
¾ teaspoon freshly ground
    black pepper
1½ cups chopped onion
1 cup grated carrot
½ pound mushrooms, sliced

3 tablespoons minced parsley
½ cup peeled, chopped
    tomatoes
½ teaspoon thyme
½ cup diced cooked ham
1 cup dry white wine
3 tablespoons butter

Fry the bacon until it begins to brown. Drain and crumble.

Cut the fillets in half. Season with 1½ teaspoons of the salt and ¼ teaspoon pepper. Spread the bacon on the bottom of a shallow greased casserole. Mix together the onion, carrot, mushrooms, parsley, tomatoes, thyme, remaining salt and pepper, and ham. Spread half the mixture over the bacon. Arrange the fish over the vegetables and cover with remaining vegetable mixture. Add the wine, and dot with the butter. Bake in a 375° oven 45 minutes.

Serves 6-8.

Serve with a white Burgundy, a dry German white wine, an Alsatian wine like Riesling, or any *rosé*.

LOBSTER AND MACARONI CASSEROLE

¼ pound (1 stick) butter
½ cup grated onion
1 clove garlic, minced
4 tablespoons flour
2 cups chicken broth
2 tablespoons tomato paste
1½ cups dry white wine
1 pound cooked lobster meat, diced

¼ cup chopped parsley
1 teaspoon salt
½ teaspoon freshly ground black pepper
1 pound elbow macaroni, cooked and drained
½ cup grated Swiss cheese
1 teaspoon paprika

Melt half the butter in a saucepan; sauté the onion and garlic 5 minutes, stirring frequently. Blend in the flour. Gradually add the broth, stirring constantly to the boiling point. Mix in the tomato paste. Cook over low heat for 15 minutes. Add the wine, lobster, parsley, salt, and pepper. Cook over low heat for 5 minutes. Mix in the macaroni and taste for seasoning.

Pour the mixture into a buttered casserole. Sprinkle with the cheese and paprika. Dot with the remaining butter. Bake in a 375° oven 20 minutes, or until lightly browned.

Serves 4-6.

Serve with a white Burgundy, champagne, a dry German white wine, or an Italian white wine like Orvieto.

TROUT WITH WINE ASPIC

4 brook trout
2 cups dry white wine
¾ cup water
1½ teaspoon salt
¼ teaspoon white pepper

1 tablespoon minced parsley
¼ teaspoon tarragon
1 envelope (tablespoon) gelatin
3 tablespoons dry sherry

Wash the trout; remove the heads if you like.

In a skillet, combine the wine, water, salt, pepper, parsley, and tarragon. Bring to a boil, and cook over low heat 10 minutes. Arrange the trout in the skillet. Bring to a boil, cover loosely, and cook over low heat 20 minutes, or until the fish flakes easily when tested with a fork. Carefully transfer the trout to a serving dish.

Soften the gelatin in the sherry, then stir into the hot stock until dissolved. Pour over the fish and chill until set. Serves 4.

Serve with a dry German white wine, or a Loire Valley wine like Pouilly-Fumé, or a *rosé*.

SPAGHETTI WITH ONIONS AND ANCHOVIES

½ cup olive oil	1 teaspoon oregano
1½ pounds onion, chopped	½ cup chopped parsley
8 anchovies, chopped	1 pound spaghetti, cooked
1 8-ounce can tomato sauce	and drained
½ cup dry white wine	

Heat the olive oil in a saucepan; sauté the chopped onions 10 minutes, stirring frequently. Mix in the anchovies, tomato sauce, wine and oregano. Cook over low heat 45 minutes. Add a little water if the sauce is too thick. Add the parsley. Taste for seasoning.

Heap the spaghetti on a platter and pour the sauce over it. Toss lightly and serve immediately.

Serves 4-6.

Serve with a dry Italian white wine like Verdicchio or Orvieto, or with a dry white Bordeaux wine.

BAKED FISH AND MACARONI

2 cups water	½ teaspoon freshly ground
1¼ cups dry white wine	black pepper
½ cup chopped carrot	½ cup heavy cream
½ cup chopped onion	1 egg yolk
2 teaspoons salt	½ pound elbow macaroni,
2 pounds white fish or	cooked and drained
sea bass	¼ cup grated Swiss cheese
2 tablespoons butter	3 tablespoons dry bread
2 tablespoons flour	crumbs
1 teaspoon salt	

Bring the water and 1 cup of the wine to a boil; add the carrot, onion, salt, and fish. Cover, and cook over low heat 15 minutes. Drain. Strain, and reserve 1½ cups stock. Remove skin and bones and cut fish into 2-inch pieces.

Melt the butter in a saucepan, blend in the flour, salt, and pepper. Add fish stock and cream, stirring steadily until sauce thickens. Beat the egg yolk and remaining wine in a bowl. Add the hot sauce, stirring steadily to prevent curdling. In a 2-quart buttered baking dish, spread a layer of macaroni, sprinkle with some grated cheese, add a layer of fish, and then a layer of sauce. Repeat until all ingredients are used up. Have the top layer macaroni. Sprinkle with the bread crumbs and bake in a preheated 400° oven 20 minutes.

Serves 6.

Serve with any dry white wine, or if you wish, with a *rosé*.

SEAFOOD KABOBS

30 scallops	¼ teaspoon dry mustard
1 cup soy sauce	¼ teaspoon thyme
2/3 cup dry red wine	1 teaspoon ground ginger
¼ cup sherry	1 teaspoon Worcestershire
½ cup pineapple juice	sauce
½ cup brown sugar	30 shrimp, cooked and
¼ cup melted butter	cleaned

Cover the scallops with water; bring to a boil and drain.

In a bowl, combine the soy sauce, red wine, sherry, pineapple juice, sugar, butter, mustard, thyme, ginger, and Worcestershire sauce. Marinate the scallops and shrimp in the mixture for 2 hours. Arrange the shrimp and scallops alternately on 6, 8 or 10 skewers.

Broil 3 minutes on each side. Serve with boiled rice and sautéed pineapple slices.

Serves 6-10.

FILETS DE POISSON EN SOUFFLE

½ cup dry vermouth	3 tablespoons flour
¼ cup sliced onion	1 cup milk, scalded
1⅛ teaspoon salt	Dash nutmeg
¼ teaspoon white pepper	1 egg yolk
½ pound fillet of sole	4 egg whites
3 tablespoons butter	½ cup grated Swiss cheese

Combine the vermouth, sliced onion, ½ teaspoon of the salt, and ¼ teaspoon pepper in a skillet. Bring to a boil, and add the fish fillets. Cover, and cook over low heat 10 minutes. Drain, and flake the fish coarsely.

Melt the butter in a saucepan; blend in the flour. Add the milk, stirring steadily to the boiling point. Add the nutmeg, ½ teaspoon of the remaining salt, and the remaining pepper; cook over low heat 5 minutes. Beat the egg yolk in a bowl; gradually add the hot sauce, stirring steadily to prevent curdling. Cool.

Beat the egg whites and remaining salt until stiff but not dry. Stir about ¼ of this into the sauce, mix in ⅓ cup of the cheese, then fold in the remaining egg whites.

Use 6 individual shallow baking dishes. Spread each with about a ¼-inch layer of the soufflé mixture. Put the fish over it and heap the remaining soufflé mixture over the fish. Sprinkle with the remaining cheese. Bake in a preheated 425° oven (on upper rack) 15 minutes, or until puffed and browned. Serve immediately.

Serves 6.

Serve with a dry white Burgundy, such as a Chablis, a dry German white wine, or a dry Italian white wine like Orvieto.

BAKED FILLET OF SOLE

1½ cups champagne or dry white wine	3 tablespoons heavy cream
2 tablespoons butter	2 teaspoons salt
2 tablespoons grated onion	1½ teaspoons white pepper
1 bay leaf	4 fillets of sole
½ cup chopped mushrooms	2 tablespoons grated Parmesan cheese
2 teaspoons chopped parsley	

Combine the champagne or white wine, butter, onion, bay leaf, mushrooms, and parsley in a saucepan. Bring to a boil, and cook over medium heat 10 minutes. Mix in the cream. Discard the bay leaf.

Sprinkle the salt and pepper on the fillets. Arrange in a buttered baking dish in a single layer. Pour the sauce over them and sprinkle with the cheese. Bake in a 375° oven 25 minutes.

Serves 4.

Serve with a dry German white wine, a white Burgundy, a dry white Bordeaux, or a *rosé*.

FILLET OF SOLE WITH MUSHROOM-HOLLANDAISE SAUCE

6 fillets of sole	2 cups Hollandaise sauce
2 teaspoons salt	(see recipe)
¼ teaspoons white pepper	½ cup whipped cream
½ cup chopped onion	½ cup chopped mushrooms
¼ cup dry white wine	½ cup minced pimientos
6 tablespoons butter	¾ cup peeled chopped
1 tablespoon flour	tomatoes

Cut each fillet in thirds lengthwise and roll up. Fasten with toothpicks if necessary. Season with salt and pepper. Arrange in a buttered baking pan; sprinkle with the chopped onion and wine. Cover with buttered aluminum foil and bake in a 350° oven 15 minutes. Transfer to a shallow ovenproof serving dish. Knead the flour in 3 tablespoons butter, and add to the wine sauce remaining in the pan. Bring to a boil, and cook until thickened. Strain. Add the Hollandaise sauce and whipped cream.

Sauté the mushrooms, pimientos, and tomatoes in the remaining butter for 5 minutes. Spread over the fish and cover with the sauce. Bake in a 400° oven 5 minutes, or until delicately browned. Serve with parsley potatoes.

Serves 6-8.

HOMARD À L'AMERICAINE
LOBSTER AMERICAINE

2 1½-pound live lobsters
3 tablespoons olive oil
1¼ teaspoons salt
½ teaspoon freshly ground
  black pepper
3 tablespoons butter
½ cup chopped onion
1 carrot, grated

3 tablespoons cognac
1 bay leaf
1 cup peeled, chopped
  tomatoes
¾ cup dry white wine
1 clove garlic, minced
½ teaspoon thyme

Have the bodies of the lobster cut into 4 pieces cross-wise and the claws cracked. Scoop out the liver (tomalley) and reserve.

Heat the oil in a skillet; add the lobster, salt, and pepper and cook 5 minutes, or until lobsters turn red. (At this point the lobster meat may be removed from the shells, if you like.)

Melt 2 tablespoons butter in a deep casserole; sauté the onion and carrot until browned. Add the lobster pieces. Heat the cognac in a ladle, pour over the lobster, and set aflame. When flames die, stir in the bay leaf, tomatoes, wine, garlic, and thyme. Cover tightly, and cook over low heat 20 minutes. Cream the remaining butter with the reserved liver and stir into the sauce. Cook 5 minutes. Taste for seasoning. If lobster meat has not been removed from the shells earlier, it may now be removed before serving, if desired.

Serves 2-4.

Serve with a white Burgundy, a Loire Valley wine like Chinon, or a *rosé*.

ARAGOSTA FRA DIAVOLO
LOBSTER IN TOMATO SAUCE

2 1½-pound live lobsters,
  or 4 African lobster tails
½ cup olive oil
¾ cup chopped onion
1 clove garlic, minced
1½ teaspoons salt
¼ teaspoon crushed dried
  red peppers

1 pound tomatoes, peeled
  and chopped
1 tablespoon tomato paste
¾ cup dry white wine
½ teaspoon oregano
2 tablespoons minced parsley

Have the lobsters cut up in the shell, the bodies in half lengthwise, and then in 3 pieces, and the claws cracked; or cut the lobster tails in 3 pieces crosswise.

Heat the oil in a large deep skillet; cook the lobster over high heat 3 minutes. Add the onion, garlic, salt, and dried peppers; cook until lobsters turn red, about 3 minutes. Mix in the tomatoes and tomato paste; cook 2 minutes. Add the wine and oregano. Cook over medium heat 10 minutes. Sprinkle with the parsley and serve.

Serves 2-4.

Serve with a white Burgundy, a dry Italian white wine like Orvieto, or, if you wish, with any Italian red wine like Chianti.

LOBSTER IN SPICY SAUCE

3 1½-pound live lobsters	3 tablespoons tomato paste
½ cup olive oil	1 teaspoon meat extract
1½ cups chopped onion	¼ teaspoon thyme
2 cloves garlic, minced	¼ teaspoon saffron
1/3 cup cognac	1 cup dry white wine
1¾ teaspoons salt	1 teaspoon prepared mustard
½ teaspoon freshly ground black pepper	2 tablespoons minced parsley

Have the lobsters cut up, bodies in thirds and claws in half. Heat the oil in a deep skillet or casserole; add the lobster pieces, and cook over high heat 5 minutes. Remove the lobster pieces and pour off half the oil. (If you like, the shells may be discarded at this point.) Sauté the onion and garlic in the oil remaining in the pan 5 minutes. Return the lobster pieces to the pan. Warm the cognac, set aflame, and pour over the lobster. When flames die, season with the salt and pepper. Mix together the tomato paste, meat extract, thyme, saffron, and wine. Mix in the lobster pieces. Cover and cook over medium heat 15 minutes. Arrange lobster pieces on a heated serving dish. Stir the mustard and parsley into the sauce. Pour over the lobster.

Serves 2-4.

Serve with a dry white Burgundy, or a *rosé*.

HOMARD AU PORTO
LOBSTER IN PORT

2 1¼-pound live lobsters   ¼ teaspoon white pepper
5 tablespoons butter   ¾ cup port
¾ cup chopped onion   2 tablespoons flour
½ cup grated carrot   ¾ cup heavy cream
1 teaspoon salt

Have the lobsters cut up, bodies in thirds and claws in half. Remove the meat of the bodies and claws, and slice. Melt 4 tablespoons butter in a saucepan; sauté the onion and carrot 5 minutes. Add the lobster meat; sauté 3 minutes, turning the pieces to coat all sides. Add the salt, pepper, and port. Cook over low heat 15 minutes. Transfer lobster to a heated serving dish and keep hot. Mix the flour and cream until smooth; add to the sauce with the remaining butter, stirring constantly to the boiling point. Cook over low heat 5 minutes. Taste for seasoning, and strain over the lobster meat.

Serves 2-4.

Serve with a white Burgundy, a dry Italian white wine, a German white wine, or a *rosé*.

HOMARD À LA NEWBURG
LOBSTER NEWBURG

4 tablespoons butter   ¼ teaspoon white pepper
1 pound cooked lobster meat,   ¾ cup sweet sherry
    sliced   4 egg yolks
1 teaspoon salt   1 cup heavy cream

Melt the butter in a deep skillet; add the lobster, salt, and pepper and sauté 2 minutes, stirring a few times. Stir in the sherry; cook over low heat until wine is almost evaporated. Just before serving, beat together the egg yolks and cream; add to the lobster, stirring steadily until thickened, but do not let boil. Taste for seasoning.

Serves 4-6.

Serve with a white Burgundy or a *rosé*.

HOMARD THERMIDOR
LOBSTER THERMIDOR

2 cups dry white wine	2 cups light cream
4 cups water	3 tablespoons dry vermouth
1 onion	¼ teaspoon chervil
1 bay leaf	¼ teaspoon dry mustard
1 stalk celery	⅛ teaspoon tarragon
3 teaspoons salt	¼ teaspoon white pepper
2 1½-pound live lobsters	1 tablespoon beef extract
¼ pound butter	4 tablespoons grated
4 tablespoons flour	Parmesan cheese

Combine the white wine, water, onion, bay leaf, celery, and 2 teaspoons salt in a saucepan; bring to a boil, and cook over low heat 20 minutes. Plunge the lobsters into boiling liquid and cook 20 minutes. Remove lobsters, drain, cool, and split. Remove the meat of the bodies and claws; slice. Reserve the body shells. Pour off all but 1 cup of the lobster stock; cook over high heat until reduced to ¼ cup.

Melt 4 tablespoons butter in a saucepan; blend in the flour and remaining salt. Gradually add the cream, stirring steadily to the boiling point. Mix in the vermouth, chervil, mustard, tarragon, pepper, beef extract, and reduced stock. Cook over low heat 5 minutes. Taste for seasoning and stir in the remaining butter. Spread a little of the sauce on the bottom of the reserved shells and arrange the lobster meat over it. Cover with remaining sauce and sprinkle with the cheese. Place under the broiler until browned.

Serves 2-4.

Serve with a white Burgundy, a Loire Valley white wine, or a *rosé*.

HOMARD AU CHAMPAGNE
LOBSTER IN CHAMPAGNE SAUCE

4 tablespoons butter	1 cup heavy cream
¾ cup sliced blanched	1 teaspoon salt
almonds	Dash cayenne pepper
2 tablespoons flour	2 pounds cooked lobster
2 cups champagne or	meat, cubed
dry white wine	1 tablespoon chopped parsley
2 egg yolks	

Melt 2 tablespoons of the butter in a skillet. Add the almonds. Sauté until brown, stirring almost constantly.

Melt the remaining butter in a saucepan. Blend in the flour until smooth. Gradually add the champagne or white wine, stirring constantly to the boiling point, then cook over low heat 5 minutes.

Beat the egg yolks, cream, salt, and cayenne pepper in a bowl. Gradually add 1 cup of the champagne sauce, beating constantly to prevent curdling. Return the mixture to the balance of the sauce. Fold in the lobster meat and almonds. Taste for seasoning. Reheat, but do not allow to boil. Sprinkle with the parsley. Serve with boiled rice.

Serves 6-8.

Serve with champagne, a dry German white wine, a white Burgundy, or any dry Italian white wine like Orvieto.

COQUILLES SAINT-JACQUES
BAKED SCALLOPS

1 pound scallops	1 teaspoon lemon juice
1½ cups water	6 tablespoons butter
¾ cup dry white wine	3 tablespoons flour
2 sprigs parsley ⎱ tied	2 egg yolks
1 bay leaf ⎰ together	4 tablespoons heavy cream
½ pound mushrooms, chopped	1¼ teaspoons salt
1 cup finely chopped onion	¼ teaspoon white pepper
2 tablespoons sherry	½ cup dry bread crumbs

Combine the scallops, 1½ cups water, the wine, parsley, and bay leaf in a saucepan; bring to a boil, and cook over low heat 5 minutes. Drain scallops, reserve the liquid. In a saucepan combine the mushrooms, onion, sherry, lemon juice, and 2 tablespoons butter. Bring to a boil, cover, and cook 10 minutes. Strain and reserve the liquid. Dice the scallops.

Melt 3 tablespoons butter in a saucepan; blend in the flour. Add the reserved liquids, stirring constantly to the boiling point. Cook over low heat 3 minutes. Beat the egg yolks and cream in a bowl, and mix in a little of the hot sauce, stirring steadily to prevent curdling. Return to balance of sauce and cook until thickened; do not allow to boil. Season with the salt and pepper. Add the scallops to sauce with the mushroom-onion mixture. Mix well, and spoon into 6 scallop shells or ramekins. Sprinkle with the bread crumbs and dot with remaining butter. Bake in a 425° oven 10 minutes.

Serves 6.

Serve with a dry white Burgundy, a Loire Valley wine like Chinon, or an Alsatian wine.

COQUILLES ST.-JACQUES MARINÉES
MARINATED BROILED SCALLOPS

1½ pounds scallops	2 cloves garlic, minced
½ cup olive oil	2 tablespoons minced parsley
½ cup dry vermouth	¾ teaspoon salt

If sea scallops are used, cut in half crosswise. If bay scallops are used, leave whole. Wash and dry. Combine the oil, vermouth, garlic, parsley, and salt in a glass or pottery bowl. Marinate the scallops in mixture 4 hours, or overnight, in the refrigerator.

Arrange scallops in a shallow pan with marinade. Broil 2 inches from heat until golden brown, turning to brown all sides.

Serves 4-6.

To serve as hot hors d'oeuvre, pierce with cocktail picks.

Serve with any dry white wine, especially an Italian white wine.

RISOTTO DI SCAMPI
SHRIMP RISOTTO

3 tablespoons olive oil	1 pound cooked shrimp, shelled and deveined
6 tablespoons butter	
1 clove garlic, minced	1½ teaspoons salt
1½ cups raw rice	¼ teaspoon white pepper
¾ cup dry white wine	¼ teaspoon marjoram
4 cups hot chicken broth	3 tablespoons grated Parmesan cheese

Heat the oil and 4 tablespoons of the butter in a heavy deep skillet or a casserole. Add the garlic and rice; cook until rice is translucent, stirring frequently. Add the wine; cook over medium heat until absorbed. Add half the broth; cover, and cook over low heat 15 minutes. Mix in the shrimp, salt, pepper, marjoram, and remaining broth. Recover, and cook 10 minutes longer, or until rice is tender and dry. Stir in the cheese and remaining butter with a fork.

Serves 4-6.

Serve with any dry white wine, especially a Loire Valley wine or a white Burgundy.

DEVILED SHRIMP

2 pounds raw shrimp, shelled and deveined	1½ teaspoons salt
	¼ teaspoon thyme
1 cup dry white wine	1 bay leaf
¼ cup cognac	2 tablespoons heavy cream
3 sprigs parsley	2 tablespoons dry sherry
1 carrot, sliced	1 cup mayonnaise
1 onion	¼ cup chopped pimiento-
1 clove garlic, split	stuffed olives

Wash and drain the shrimp. Combine the wine, cognac, parsley, carrot, onion, garlic, salt, thyme, and bay leaf in a saucepan. Bring to a boil, add the shrimp, and cook over low heat 8 minutes. Let cool in the liquid. Drain thoroughly.

Blend the cream and sherry with the mayonnaise; fold in the chopped olives. Arrange the shrimp on a platter or on individual dishes and cover with the mayonnaise mixture. Or if you want to serve the shrimp as an hors d'eouvre, serve the mayonnaise mixture as a dip.

Serves 4-6.

Serve with a dry white Burgundy, a dry German white wine, or a Loire Valley wine like Pouilly-Fumé.

POISSON AUX OLIVES
FISH WITH OLIVES

2 pounds sea bass or   ¼ teaspoon thyme
   mackerel, split   ⅛ teaspoon finely chopped
1½ teaspoons salt   bay leaf
¼ teaspoon white pepper   ½ cup pitted black olives
¼ cup olive oil   Orange slices
¼ cup dry white wine

Wash and dry the fish. Season with the salt and pepper.
Rub a baking dish with a little oil and arrange the fish in
it. Pour the oil and wine over it, and sprinkle with the
thyme and bay leaf. Bake in a 375° oven 20 minutes, basting occasionally. Add the olives and bake 5 minutes longer.
Garnish with orange slices. Serve hot or cold.

Serves 4.

Serve with a white Burgundy, a white Rhône wine like
Châteauneuf-du-Pape Blanc, a dry Italian white wine like
Soave, or a rosé.

FILETS DE MAQUEREAUX AU VIN BLANC
MACKEREL IN WHITE WINE

2 2-pound mackerel, filleted   1 bay leaf
1½ cups dry white wine   ⅛ teaspoon fennel
¼ cup water   1 teaspoon prepared French
¾ cup sliced onion   mustard
1¼ teaspoons salt   2 tablespoons minced parsley
6 peppercorns

Remove all the bones of the fish; wash and dry. Cut
each fillet in half lengthwise, and then crosswise.

In a skillet, combine and bring to a boil the wine, water,
sliced onion, salt, peppercorns, bay leaf, and fennel. Cook
over low heat 15 minutes. Arrange the fish in it; cook
over low heat 10 minutes. Cool the fish for 15 minutes in
the stock, then transfer fish to a deep dish. Strain the liquid
and measure 1 cup; mix in the mustard and parsley. Pour
over the fish. Chill 24 hours before serving.

Serves 4-6.

Serve with a white Burgundy, a white Rhône wine like
Hermitage Blanc, a dry Italian white wine like Orvieto,
or a rosé.

SHERRIED TUNA

4 tablespoons butter	½ cup dry sherry
3 tablespoons grated onion	2 7¾-ounce cans tuna fish,
4 tablespoons flour	drained and flaked
2 cups milk	½ cup sliced pimiento-stuffed
1 teaspoon salt	olives
¼ teaspoon white pepper	

Melt the butter in a saucepan; sauté the grated onion 3 minutes. Blend in the flour. Gradually add the milk, stirring steadily to the boiling point. Stir in the salt, pepper, and sherry; cook over low heat 5 minutes. Add the tuna fish and sliced olives; cook 3 minutes. Taste for seasoning. Serve on rice or toast, or in patty shells.

Serves 6.

Serve with a *rosé* wine.

POACHED SALMON STEAK

2 tablespoons butter	½ cup dry white wine
½ cup chopped onion	2 teaspoons salt
1/3 cup gated carrot	¼ teaspoon white pepper
1/3 cup chopped celery	1 bay leaf
3 cups water	1 3-pound salmon steak

Melt the butter in a large skillet; sauté the onion, carrot, and celery 5 minutes. Add the water, wine, salt, pepper, and bay leaf; bring to a boil, and cook 5 minutes. Carefully lower the salmon into the liquid. Cover loosely, and cook over low heat 40 minutes. Remove the salmon carefully, and serve hot with Hollandaise sauce, or cold with mayonnaise.

Serves 6.

BAKED SALMON STEAKS

4 slices salmon, 1 inch thick	¼ cup grated carrot
2 teaspoons salt	2 tablespoons flour
½ teaspoon freshly ground	2 cups dry white wine
black pepper	1 bay leaf
3 tablespoons butter	3 sprigs parsley
¾ cup chopped onion	

Wash and dry the fish. If the slices are large, cut each in half through the bone. Season with the salt and pepper. In a large skillet, melt the butter. Sauté the onion and carrot 5 minutes. Blend in the flour; gradually add the wine, stirring steadily to the boiling point. If skillet has an ovenproof handle, arrange the fish in it. If not, pour the sauce into a baking dish and arrange the fish in it. Add the bay leaf and parsley. Cover the fish with a piece of buttered aluminum foil. Bake in a 400° oven 40 minutes, or until fish flakes easily when tested with a fork. Transfer the fish to a heated serving dish. Taste the sauce for seasoning, and pour over the fish.

Serves 4.

Serve with a white burgundy or Bordeaux wine, a dry German white wine, or a *rosé*.

BAKED STUFFED RED SNAPPER

1 4-pound red snapper, split and boned for stuffing	3 cups dry bread crumbs
2 teaspoons salt	1 cup chopped cucumber
½ teaspoon freshly ground black pepper	2 teaspoons capers
	¼ teaspoon marjoram
⅜ pound (1½ sticks) butter	½ cup dry white wine
¾ cup chopped onion	6 slices bacon

Sprinkle the fish inside and out with 1½ teaspoons of the salt and ¼ teaspoon pepper.

Heat half the butter in a skillet; sauté the chopped onion 5 minutes. Mix in the bread crumbs, cucumber, capers, marjoram, half the wine, and remaining salt and pepper. Stuff the fish, and close opening with skewers or toothpicks.

Place the fish in a buttered shallow baking pan. Cut 6 gashes on the top and place a piece of bacon in each. Dot with the remaining butter, and pour the remaining wine over the top.

Bake in a 400° oven 5 minutes, or until the fish flakes easily when tested with a fork. Baste frequently with the pan juices.

Serves 6.

MORUE EN VIN ROUGE
SALT COD IN RED WINE

2 pounds salt cod	½ teaspoon freshly ground
½ cup flour	black pepper
¾ cup olive oil	1 bay leaf
¾ cup finely chopped onion	¼ teaspoon thyme
1½ cups dry red wine	2 tablespoons minced parsley
1 cup water	2 tablespoons capers
1 tablespoon tomato paste	

Wash the codfish, cover with cold water, and let soak 12 hours, changing the water a few times. Drain, cover with fresh water, and bring to a boil. Drain, remove the skin and bones, and cut fish into squares. Roll the squares in the flour (reserving 1½ tablespoons). Heat ½ cup of the oil in a skillet; brown the squares in it. Pour off the oil and set fish aside. Wipe the skillet clean with paper towels.

Heat the remaining oil in the skillet; sauté the onion 10 minutes. Blend in the reserved flour until golden. Add the wine and water, stirring steadily to the boiling point. Mix in the tomato paste, pepper, bay leaf, thyme, and parsley. Bring to a boil, and cook over low heat 30 minutes. Add the codfish and capers; cook 15 minutes longer. Taste for seasoning, discard the bay leaf, and serve on sautéed bread slices or boiled rice.

Serves 6-8.

Serve with a red Burgundy like Beaujolais, a dry white Burgundy, or a *rosé*.

ANGUILLES, SAUCE VERT
EELS IN GREEN SAUCE

1½ pounds eels	¼ teaspoon freshly ground
½ cup olive oil	black pepper
2 cups boiling chicken broth	¼ cup cooked puréed spinach
1 cup dry white wine	¼ cup chopped parsley
2 tablespoons lemon juice	¼ cup chopped mint
1 teaspoon salt	¼ cup chopped chives

Clean the eels, remove the skin, and cut in 1½-inch lengths.

Heat the oil in a skillet; sauté the eels 5 minutes. Add the broth, and cook 5 minutes longer. Drain.

Combine the eels, wine, lemon juice, salt, pepper, spinach, parsley, mint, and chives. Bring to a boil. Cool, and chill.

Serves 8-10.

Poultry

POLLO ALLA CACCIATORA
CHICKEN IN RED WINE, HUNTER'S STYLE

5-pound roasting chicken, disjointed
¼ cup olive oil
¾ cup chopped onion
¾ cup thinly sliced green peppers
1 clove garlic, minced
1½ teaspoons salt
½ teaspoon black pepper
¼ teaspoon rosemary
¾ cup peeled, chopped tomatoes
1 cup dry red wine
¼ pound mushrooms, sliced
2 tablespoons butter

Wash and dry the chicken pieces. Heat the oil in a Dutch oven or deep skillet; brown the chicken in it. Mix in the onion, green peppers, garlic, salt, pepper, and rosemary; cook 10 minutes. Mix in the tomatoes and wine; bring to a boil, cover, and cook over low heat 30 minutes. Sauté the mushrooms in the butter 5 minutes. Add to the chicken; re-cover, and cook 10 minutes longer, or until the chicken is tender. Taste for seasoning.

Serves 4-6.

Serve with an Italian red wine like Chianti, a red Bordeaux, or a red Burgundy, especially Beaujolais.

POULET AU CHAMPAGNE
CHICKEN IN CHAMPAGNE

2 teaspoons salt
½ teaspoon freshly ground black pepper
4-pound pullet, disjointed
4 tablespoons butter
3 tablespoons warmed cognac
¼ cup chopped shallots or green onions
1 cup champagne
1 tomato, peeled and chopped
½ teaspoon paprika
½ teaspoon tarragon
1 egg yolk
¼ cup heavy cream

Rub the salt and pepper into the chicken. Melt the butter in a heavy saucepan or Dutch oven; brown the chicken in it. Set the cognac aflame and pour over the chicken. Add the shallots, champagne, tomato, paprika, and tarragon. Cover, and cook over low heat for 1 hour, or until chicken is tender.

Beat together the egg yolk and cream in a bowl. Pour off most of the sauce from the chicken, and gradually add it to the egg-yolk mixture, beating constantly to prevent curdling. Return to chicken. Reheat, but do not allow to boil.

Arrange the chicken on a hot platter. Pour the sauce over it. Serve with boiled potatoes and sautéed mushrooms. Serves 4-6.

Serve with champagne, a white Burgundy, or any dry Italian white wine.

POLLO EN SALSA DE VINO
CHICKEN IN WINE SAUCE

5-pound roasting chicken, disjointed	1 clove garlic, minced
1/3 cup flour	½ teaspoon thyme
2 teaspoons salt	2 tablespoons minced parsley
½ teaspoon freshly ground black pepper	1½ cups dry white wine
3 tablespoons olive oil	2 cups cooked or canned green peas
1 cup chopped onion	3 pimientos, cut julienne
	½ teaspoon saffron

Wash and dry the chicken pieces; roll in a mixture of the flour, salt, and pepper. Heat the oil in a Dutch oven or deep skillet; add the chicken, onion, and garlic. Cook until chicken is browned. Add the thyme, parsley, and wine. Bring to a boil, cover, and cook over low heat 45 minutes. Add the peas, pimientos, and saffron; cook 10 minutes longer, or until the chicken is tender.

Serves 4-6.

Serve with a white Burgundy or Bordeaux, champagne, a Loire Valley wine like Pouilly-Fumé, an Alsatian wine like Traminer, or a *rosé*.

COQ AU VIN BLANC
CHICKEN IN WHITE WINE SAUCE

2 2½-pound fryers,
    quartered
¼ cup flour
2 teaspoons salt
½ teaspoon freshly ground
    black pepper
¼ cup olive oil
¾ cup chopped onion
½ cup grated carrot
2 cloves garlic, minced

2 teaspoons finely chopped
    bay leaves
3 tablespoons minced parsley
¼ teaspoon thyme
3 cups dry white wine
½ pound mushrooms, sliced
3 tablespoons butter
2 cloves
12 small white onions

Wash and dry the chicken. Dip in a mixture of the flour, salt, and pepper. Heat the oil in a deep skillet or casserole; brown the chicken in it. Add the chopped onion, carrot, and garlic; cook 10 minutes, stirring frequently. Add the bay leaves, parsley, thyme, and wine. Bring to a boil, cover, and cook over medium heat 10 minutes.

Sauté the mushrooms in the butter 5 minutes. Stick the cloves in one of the white onions. Add the onions and mushrooms to the pan. Re-cover, and cook over low heat 20 minutes, or until chicken is tender. (If sauce is too thin, thicken with 1 tablespoon flour kneaded with 1 tablespoon butter.)

Serves 6-8.

Serve with a dry white Burgundy or Bordeaux, a dry German white wine, a Loire Valley wine like Pouilly-Fumé, or a *rosé*.

COQ AU VIN ROUGE
CHICKEN IN RED WINE

¼ pound bacon
6 tablespoons butter
3-pound fryer, disjointed
1½ teaspoons salt
¼ teaspoons freshly ground
    black pepper
¼ cup warmed cognac
3 cups dry red wine
1 clove garlic, minced

2 teaspoons tomato paste
1 teaspoon finely chopped
    bay leaf
¼ teaspoon thyme
12 small white onions
½ cup boiling water
12 mushroom caps
1 tablespoon cornstarch
2 tablespoons dry sherry

Cook the bacon in boiling water 10 minutes. Drain and dry. In a casserole or Dutch oven, brown the bacon. Remove bacon, crumble, and set aside; pour off all but 1 tablespoon fat. Add 2 tablespoons butter to the fat; brown the chicken in it. Season with the salt and pepper. Set the cognac aflame, and pour it over the chicken. When flames die, add the wine, garlic, tomato paste, bay leaf, thyme, and bacon bits. Cover, and cook over low heat 30 minutes, or until chicken is tender.

While the chicken is cooking, prepare the vegetables. Melt 2 tablespoons butter in a skillet; sauté the onions until browned, shaking the pan frequently. Add the boiling water; cover, and cook over low heat 20 minutes. Season with salt and pepper. Sauté the mushrooms in the remaining butter 5 minutes.

Skim the fat from the chicken gravy. Mix the cornstarch with the sherry; stir into the gravy until thickened. Add the onions and mushrooms, and taste for seasoning. Cover, and cook over low heat 10 minutes.

Serves 4-5.

Serve with a red Bordeaux, a red Burgundy like Beaujolais, an Italian red wine like Valpolicella, or a *rosé*.

LIQUORED CHICKEN

3½-pound fryer, disjointed	¼ cup cognac
1½ teaspoons salt	¼ cup bourbon
¼ teaspoon white pepper	¼ cup port or sweet sherry
¼ pound butter	2 egg yolks
2 tablespoons olive oil	2 cups heavy cream

Rub the chicken pieces with the salt and pepper. Heat 3 tablespoons butter and the olive oil in a skillet; cook the chicken in it until browned and tender. Transfer to a covered hot dish and place in a 325° oven while preparing the sauce.

Drain the fat from the skillet. Into the skillet, stir the cognac, bourbon, and port, scraping the bottom for any browned particles. Cook over low heat until reduced to approximately ⅓ original amount.

Beat the egg yolks with the heavy cream. Place over

very low heat until it begins to thicken slightly, stirring steadily. Add the remaining butter. Blend in the liquors, taste for seasoning, and pour over chicken. Do not allow sauce to boil. Serve with rice.

Serves 4.

Serve with a white Burgundy, or a *rosé*.

STUFFED CHICKEN IN SHERRY

½ pound chicken livers	3 teaspoons salt
6 tablespoons butter	¾ teaspoon freshly ground
¼ pound ham, cut julienne	black pepper
3 pimientos, cut julienne	6-pound roasting chicken
2 hard-cooked egg yolks,	or capon
chopped	1 teaspoon vinegar
1 teaspoon paprika	¾ cup dry sherry

Wash the livers, removing any discolored areas. Cut each liver in quarters. Melt 2 tablespoons butter in a skillet; sauté the livers 5 minutes. Mix in the ham, pimientos, chopped egg yolks, paprika, 1 teaspoon of the salt, and ¼ teaspoon pepper. Rub the chicken with the remaining salt and pepper; stuff with the liver mixture. Close the opening with skewers, thread, or aluminum foil, and truss.

Melt the remaining butter in a roasting pan; place the chicken in it. Roast in a 375° oven 2¼ hours, or until tender, basting occasionally. Transfer the chicken to a heated platter. Place the pan over direct heat and stir in the vinegar and sherry. Bring to a boil, scraping the bottom of any browned particles. Pour over the chicken.

Serves 4-6.

Serve with a red Bordeaux, a dry white Burgundy, an Italian dry white wine like Verdicchio, an Alsatian wine like Riesling, or a *rosé*.

BRAISED PULLET IN WINE CREAM

4-pound pullet, disjointed	1 bay leaf ⎫ tied
2 tablespoons butter	3 sprigs parsley ⎬ together
1½ teaspoons salt	¼ teaspoon thyme
¼ teaspoon white pepper	12 mushroom caps, sautéed
½ cup chopped onion	½ cup heavy cream, scalded
¾ cup dry white wine	1 tablespoon lemon juice
2 tablespoons dry sherry	1 truffle, sliced

Wash and dry the chicken pieces. Melt the butter in a deep skillet; add the chicken, salt, pepper, and chopped onion. Cover the pan, and cook over low heat 25 minutes, turning the chicken pieces several times. Add the wine, sherry, bay leaf, parsley, and thyme, and cook 15 minutes longer, or until chicken is tender. Discard bay leaf and parsley. Arrange chicken on a hot serving dish and garnish with mushrooms. Add the cream and lemon juice to the pan juices. Bring to a boil, and strain sauce over the chicken. Garnish with the truffle.

Serves 4.

Serve with a dry German white wine, a white Bordeaux or Burgundy, a dry Italian white wine, or a *rosé*.

POLLO AL CAZADOR
CHICKEN IN WINE, HUNTER'S STYLE

2 3-pound fryers, disjointed	½ cup mushrooms, sliced
½ cup flour	1 cup sliced green peppers
2½ teaspoons salt	1 bay leaf
½ teaspoon freshly ground black pepper	½ teaspoon oregano
	⅛ teaspoon dried ground red peppers
1/3 cup olive oil	
8 small white onions	1½ cups dry red wine
1 cup peeled, chopped tomatoes	1½ cups drained canned chick-peas

Wash and dry the chicken pieces; roll in a mixture of the flour, salt, and black pepper. Heat the oil in a casserole or Dutch oven; brown the chicken in it. Add the onions, tomatoes, and mushrooms; cook over medium heat 10 minutes, stirring frequently. Add the green peppers, bay leaf, oregano, dried red peppers, wine, and chick-peas. Bring to a boil, cover, and cook over low heat 45 minutes, or until chicken is tender. Taste for seasoning.

Serves 6-8.

Serve with a red Bordeaux, a red Burgundy, especially a Beaujolais, or a red Italian wine like Bardolino.

POULET MARENGO
CHICKEN MARENGO

2 2½-pound broilers, disjointed
½ cup flour
2½ teaspoons salt
¾ teaspoon freshly ground black pepper
2 tablespoons olive oil
2 tablespoons butter
3 cloves garlic
1 cup dry white wine

2 tablespoons cognac
1 cup peeled, diced tomatoes
1 bay leaf
¼ teaspoon marjoram
½ pound mushrooms, quartered
¼ cup sliced stuffed green olives
2 tablespoons minced parsley

Wash and dry the chicken pieces; toss in a mixture of the flour, salt and pepper. Heat the olive oil and butter in a casserole; brown the chicken in it. Add the garlic, wine, cognac, tomatoes, bay leaf, and marjoram. Bring to a boil, cover, and cook over low heat 25 minutes. Add the mushrooms and olives; cook 10 minutes longer, or until chicken is tender. Taste for seasoning, sprinkle with parsley, and garnish with sautéed French bread slices around the edges.

Serves 6-8.

Serve with a white Burgundy or Bordeaux, a Loire Valley wine like Chinon, or a dry German white or Italian white wine.

POLLO ALLA SICILIANA
SAUTÉED CHICKEN WITH EGGPLANT

¾ pound small white
onions, peeled
3½-pound fryer, disjointed
2 tablespoons butter
1/3 cup olive oil
2½ teaspoons salt
½ teaspoon black pepper
1 clove garlic, minced

¾ cup Marsala or
sweet sherry
1 cup peeled, diced tomatoes
3 tablespoons minced parsley
1 small eggplant,
peeled and sliced
1/3 cup flour

Cook the onions in boiling water 5 minutes; drain and dry. Wash and dry the chicken. Heat the butter and 3 tablespoons of the oil in a skillet; brown the chicken and onions in it. Add 1½ teaspoons of the salt, the pepper, garlic, and wine; cook over medium heat until almost all the wine is evaporated. Mix in the tomatoes and parsley. Cover, and cook over low heat 30 minutes, or until chicken is tender. Taste for seasoning.

While the chicken is cooking, dip the eggplant slices in the flour, then sauté in the remaining oil until browned on both sides. Sprinkle with the remaining salt. Arrange the eggplant slices on a heated platter, with the chicken over it.

Serves 4.

Serve with a dry Italian white wine like Soave, a white Burgundy, a dry German white wine, or a *rosé*.

POULET À LA NIÇOISE
CHICKEN WITH TOMATOES AND OLIVES

3 tablespoons olive oil
2 tablespoons butter
5-pound roasting chicken,
disjointed
2 teaspoons salt
½ teaspoon freshly ground
black pepper
1 teaspoon saffron
3 cloves garlic, minced

1 teaspoon finely crushed
bay leaves
¼ teaspoon thyme
2½ cups peeled, diced
tomatoes
1½ cups dry white wine
1 cup water
½ cup pitted green olives
½ cup pitted black olives

Heat the olive oil and butter in a casserole; brown the chicken in it. Sprinkle with the salt, pepper, and saffron, and add the garlic, bay leaves, thyme, tomatoes, wine, and water. Bring to a boil, cover, and cook over low heat 1 hour, or until chicken is tender. Add the olives. Taste for seasoning, and cook 10 minutes longer.

Serves 4-6.

Serve with a white Burgundy, an Alsatian wine like Riesling, or a Loire Valley wine like Pouilly-Fumé or a *rosé*.

POLLO EN SALSA DE HUEVOS
CHICKEN IN EGG SAUCE

2 3-pound fryers, disjointed	1 cup water
2½ teaspoons salt	3 eggs
½ teaspoon freshly ground	3 tablespoons lemon juice
black pepper	1½ teaspoons dry mustard
4 tablespoons butter	1 teaspoon sugar
1½ cups dry white wine	

Wash and dry the chicken; rub with the salt and pepper. Melt the butter in a casserole; brown the chicken in it. Add the wine and water; cover, and cook over low heat 45 minutes or until tender.

Beat the eggs, lemon juice, mustard, and sugar in the top of a double boiler. Place over hot water and cook, stirring steadily until thickened. Add the gravy from the chicken to the mixture, and pour over the chicken. Cook over low heat, basting steadily until chicken is well coated.

Serves 6-8.

Serve with a white Burgundy, a dry German white wine, a Loire Valley wine like Sancerre, or a *rosé*.

POULARDE À L'ESTRAGON
CHICKEN WITH TARRAGON

4-pound pullet	Bunch of tarragon, or 1½
2 teaspoons salt	teaspoon dried tarragon
½ teaspoon freshly ground	6 tablespoons butter
black pepper	½ cup dry white wine

Clean, wash, and dry the chicken; rub with the salt and pepper. Place ¾ of the bunch of tarragon or 1 teaspoon dried tarragon in the cavity; truss the chicken.

Melt the butter in a small shallow roasting pan; place the chicken in it. Roast in a 375° oven 1½ hours, or until chicken is tender. Baste frequently. Remove chicken from oven and transfer to a heated platter. Stir the wine and the remaining tarragon into the pan; cook over direct heat, scraping the bottom of the pan, until mixture boils; then cook 2 minutes. Carve the chicken and pour the wine sauce over it.

Serves 4-5.

Serve with a white Burgundy, a dry German white wine, or, if you wish, with a *rosé*.

POULARDE BASQUAISE
CHICKEN, BASQUE STYLE

5-pound roasting chicken, disjointed
2 teaspoons salt
½ teaspoon freshly ground black pepper
¼ cup olive oil
2 tablespoons butter
8 small white onions
½ pound mushrooms, sliced
2 cups peeled, diced eggplant
2 cloves garlic, minced
1 cup finely sliced green peppers
3 tomatoes, peeled and quartered
2 teaspoons finely crushed bay leaves
½ teaspoon basil
½ teaspoon thyme
¾ cup dry white wine

Rub the chicken pieces with the salt and pepper. Heat the oil in a skillet; brown the chicken in it. Transfer to a casserole. Add the butter to the oil remaining in the skillet, sauté the onions 5 minutes. Mix the mushrooms, eggplant, garlic, green peppers, tomatoes, bay leaves, basil, and thyme. Sauté 5 minutes. Spread around the chicken. Stir the wine into the skillet and scrape the bottom of any browned particles; pour over the chicken mixture. Bring to a boil, cover, and bake in a 350° oven 50 minutes, or until chicken is tender. Taste for seasoning.

Serves 4.

Serve with a white Burgundy, an Alsatian wine, or a dry German white wine.

POLLO PIQUANTE
CHICKEN IN SPICY SAUCE

2 2½-pound fryers, disjointed

2 teaspoons salt

¾ teaspoon freshly ground black pepper

3 tablespoons flour

4 tablespoons olive oil

1 cup chopped onion

1½ cups dry white wine

1 tablespoon tomato paste

½ cup chicken broth

¾ cup wine vinegar

2 teaspoons anchovy paste

2 cloves garlic, minced

1 tablespoon capers

3 tablespoons chopped sweet pickles

2 tablespoons chopped parsley

Wash and dry the chicken pieces; rub with a mixture of the salt, pepper, and flour. Heat the oil in a casserole; sauté the onion 5 minutes. Add the chicken, and cook until browned. Stir in the wine, tomato paste, and broth. Cover, and cook over medium heat 45 minutes, or until chicken is tender.

In a small saucepan, cook the vinegar over high heat until reduced to half. Add the anchovy paste, garlic, capers, pickles, and parsley. Cook 1 minute; pour over the chicken and serve.

Serves 6-8.

Serve with a white Burgundy, a white Rhône wine like Hermitage Blanc, a dry Italian white like Orvieto, or a *rosé*.

POLLO CON PAN
CHICKEN WITH BREAD CRUMBS

4-pound roasting chicken, disjointed

¼ cup flour

2 teaspoons salt

½ teaspoon freshly ground black pepper

4 tablespoons olive oil

1 cup diced onion

2 cloves garlic, minced

1½ cups dry white wine

½ cup hot chicken broth

1 teaspoon finely chopped bay leaf

¼ teaspoon marjoram

¼ cup ground almonds

½ teaspoon saffron

2 tablespoons butter

½ cup fresh fine bread crumbs

2 hard-cooked eggs, chopped

Wash and dry the chicken; roll in a mixture of the flour, salt, and pepper. Heat the oil in a Dutch oven or deep skillet; lightly brown the chicken in it. Add the onion and garlic; cook 5 minutes. Mix in the wine; cook over high heat 10 minutes. Add the broth, bay leaf, and marjoram. Cover, and cook over low heat 30 minutes. Mix in the almonds and saffron; re-cover, and cook 20 minutes longer, or until chicken is tender.

Melt the butter in a skillet; lightly brown the bread crumbs in it. Sprinkle the chicken with the bread crumbs and chopped eggs just before serving.

Serves 4.

Serve with any white Burgundy, a *rosé*, or any dry Italian white wine like Verdicchio or Soave.

POLLO CON FRUTAS
CHICKEN WITH FRUIT

2 3-pound fryers, disjointed	½ cup ground blanched almonds
2½ teaspoons salt	
½ teaspoon white pepper	1½ cups orange juice
4 tablespoons butter	1 cup sweet sherry
1½ cups shredded canned pineapple	¼ teaspoon cinnamon
	¼ teaspoon mace
¾ cup seedless raisins	

Wash and dry the chicken pieces; season with the salt and pepper. Melt the butter in a Dutch oven or casserole; brown the chicken in it. Add the pineapple, raisins, almonds, orange juice, sherry, cinnamon, and mace. Bring to a boil, cover, and cook over low heat 45 minutes, or until chicken is tender. Taste for seasoning.

Serves 6-8.

Serve with a light red Bordeaux, a white Burgundy, or a dry Italian white wine like Orvieto.

POULET EN CASSEROLE
CASSEROLE OF CHICKEN

5-pound roasting chicken,
    disjointed
2 teaspoons salt
½ teaspoon freshly ground
    black pepper
1 teaspoon paprika
4 tablespoons olive oil
2 tablespoons butter

½ cup sliced carrot
¾ cup diced onion
1 clove garlic, minced
½ cup julienne-cut ham
½ teaspoon marjoram
1 bay leaf
1¼ cups dry white wine
2 tablespoons cognac

Season the chicken pieces with the salt, pepper, and paprika. Heat the oil in a casserole. Brown the chicken pieces in it. Pour off the oil. Add the butter, carrot, onion, garlic, ham, marjoram, and bay leaf. Cook over low heat 5 minutes, stirring frequently. Mix in the wine, cover, and cook 35 minutes over low heat, or until chicken is tender. Season to taste. Warm the cognac and pour over the chicken. Set aflame and serve at once.

Serves 4-6.

Serve with a white Burgundy, a dry German white wine, a dry Italian white wine like white Chianti, or a rosé.

CHICKEN-NOODLE CASSEROLE À LA REINE

6 tablespoons butter
½ cup chopped onion
¼ pound mushrooms, sliced
¼ cup chopped green pepper
2 tablespoons flour
1½ cups hot chicken broth
1¼ cups light cream
2 egg yolks
1 teaspoon salt

¼ teaspoon freshly ground
    black pepper
½ cup dry sherry
3 cups diced cooked chicken
½ pound medium noodles,
    cooked and drained
½ cup grated Parmesan
    cheese

Melt 4 tablespoons of the butter in a skillet; sauté the onion, mushrooms, and green pepper 5 minutes, stirring frequently. Blend in the flour; add the broth and cream, stirring steadily to the boiling point, then cook over low heat 5 minutes.

Beat the egg yolks in a bowl with the salt, pepper, and sherry; gradually add the hot sauce, stirring steadily to prevent curdling. Mix in the chicken and noodles. Taste for seasoning. Turn into a 3-quart casserole; sprinkle with the cheese and dot with the remaining butter. Bake in a pre-heated 350° oven 25 minutes, or until top is browned.

Serves 4-6.

Serve with a rather light red Bordeaux, or a German white wine.

POLLO EN SALSA DE ALMENDRAS
CHICKEN AND ALMOND CASSEROLE

5-pound roasting chicken, disjointed
2 teaspoons salt
½ teaspoon freshly ground black pepper
¼ cup olive oil
1 cup chopped onion

1 clove garlic, minced
¾ cup chicken broth
¾ cup dry sherry
2 tablespoons lemon juice
1 cup finely ground blanched almonds

Season the chicken with the salt and pepper. Heat the oil in a casserole; brown the chicken in it. Add the onion and garlic; cook 10 minutes, stirring frequently. Mix in the broth, sherry, and lemon juice. Cover, and cook over low heat 45 minutes. Blend in the almonds. Re-cover, and cook 15 minutes longer, or until chicken is tender.

Serves 6-8.

Serve with a white Burgundy, a dry Italian white like Verdicchio, a dry German white wine, or a *rosé*.

CHICKEN IN ALMOND SAUCE

2 teaspoons salt
¼ teaspoon freshly ground black pepper
2 2½-pound fryers, disjointed
¼ pound butter
3 tablespoons cognac

3 tomatoes, peeled and chopped
1½ cups champagne or dry white wine
1 cup ground almonds
½ cup heavy cream

Sprinkle the salt and pepper on the chicken parts.

Melt the butter (reserving 2 tablespoons) in a heavy saucepan. Brown the chicken parts in it on both sides. Add the cognac and tomatoes. Cook over medium heat for 5

minutes. Mix the champagne or white wine and ½ cup of
the almonds. Cover, and cook over low heat 40 minutes,
or until the chicken is tender. Stir in the cream. Taste for
seasoning.

Arrange the chicken in a buttered casserole. Pour the
sauce over it, and sprinkle with the remaining almonds.
Dot with the reserved 2 tablespoons of butter. Bake in a
400° oven for 15 minutes, or until delicately browned on
top.

Serves 6-8.

Serve with champagne, a white Burgundy, or, if you
wish, with a *rosé*.

FRICASSEE AU VIN BLANC
FRENCH FRICASSEE IN WHITE WINE

4-pound pullet, disjointed	1 bay leaf
2½ teaspoons salt	1 clove garlic, minced
½ teaspoon freshly ground	¼ teaspoon thyme
black pepper	2 sprigs parsley
3 tablespoons flour	2 egg yolks
4 tablespoons butter	4 tablespoons heavy cream
1½ cups dry white wine	2 teaspoons lemon juice
½ cup chicken broth	

Rub the chicken with the salt, pepper, and flour. Melt
the butter in a casserole or Dutch oven, and brown the
chicken well. Stir in the wine, broth, bay leaf, garlic,
thyme, and parsley. Bring to a boil over direct heat. Cover,
and bake in a 350° oven 45 minutes, or until chicken is
tender. Remove chicken. Remove bay leaf and parsley and
discard.

Beat the egg yolks, cream, and lemon juice in a bowl.
Mix in a little of the hot sauce, stirring constantly to prevent curdling. Pour into the casserole, stirring until well
mixed. Taste for seasoning. Return the chicken to casserole
and reheat, but do not boil.

Serves 4.

Serve with a dry German white wine, a dry Italian white
wine like Soave, or a *rosé*.

ITALIAN CHICKEN FRICASSEE

4-pound pullet, disjointed
¼ cup flour
¼ cup olive oil
1 cup chopped onion
1 cup dry white wine
1 clove garlic, minced
2 anchovy fillets, minced

2 tablespoons minced capers
¼ cup ground almonds
½ cup chopped parsley
2 teaspoons salt
½ teaspoon black pepper
1 teaspoon marjoram

Wash and dry the chicken pieces; roll in the flour. Heat the oil in a Dutch oven or heavy saucepan; brown the chicken in it. Remove the chicken, and in the fat remaining, brown the chopped onion. Return the chicken; add the wine, and cook over medium heat 10 minutes. Pound the garlic, anchovies, capers, nuts, parsley, salt, pepper, and marjoram to a paste. Mix into the pan, turning the chicken a few times to coat the pieces. Cover, and cook over low heat 45 minutes, or until chicken is tender. If necessary, add small amounts of boiling water from time to time to keep chicken from burning.

Serves 4.

Serve with a white Burgundy, a dry Italian white wine like Soave, a dry German white wine, or a *rosé*.

POLLO CON PEPERONI
CHICKEN WITH PEPPERS

5-pound roasting chicken,
   disjointed
¼ cup flour
2 teaspoons salt
½ teaspoon freshly ground
   black pepper
4 tablespoons butter
½ cup finely chopped onion

¼ cup julienne-cut ham
¾ cup dry white wine
¼ teaspoon rosemary
1 cup peeled, chopped
   tomatoes
2 tablespoons olive oil
2 green peppers, cut julienne
1 clove garlic, minced

Rub the chicken pieces with a mixture of the flour, salt, and pepper. Melt 2 tablespoons butter in a skillet (with ovenproof handle) ; brown the chicken in it. Remove. Melt the remaining butter in the skillet; sauté the onion and ham 5 minutes. Return the chicken to skillet and add the wine and rosemary; cook over low heat until wine is absorbed. Add the tomatoes. Cover and bake in a 350° oven 45 minutes.

While the chicken is baking, heat the oil in a skillet; sauté the green peppers 10 minutes. Add to the chicken, with the garlic. Re-cover, and bake 15 minutes longer. Taste for seasoning.

Serves 4-5.

Serve with a dry white Bordeaux or Burgundy, a dry German white wine, an Alsatian white like Traminer, or a *rosé*.

POLLO CON FUNGHI
CHICKEN AND MUSHROOMS

3½-pound fryer, disjointed	1 cup dry white wine
½ cup flour	1 cup peeled, diced tomatoes
2½ teaspoons salt	¼ teaspoon thyme
½ teaspoon freshly ground black pepper	½ pound mushrooms, sliced
	3 tablespoons butter
¼ cup olive oil	2 tablespoons minced parsley
1 clove garlic, minced	

Roll the chicken pieces in a mixture of the flour, 2 teaspoons of the salt, and the pepper. Heat the oil in a heavy skillet; brown the chicken in it. Add the garlic, wine, tomatoes, and thyme. Cover, and cook over low heat 20 minutes, or until the chicken is tender. While the chicken is cooking, sauté the mushrooms and remaining salt in the butter. Add to the chicken just before serving. Sprinkle with the parsley.

Serves 4.

Serve with a white Burgundy, a dry German white wine, a dry Italian white wine like Orvieto, or a *rosé*.

CHICKEN WITH MUSHROOMS IN CREAM SAUCE

2 3½-pound fryers, disjointed	½ cup chopped onion
½ cup flour	½ pound mushrooms, sliced
2 teaspoons salt	2 tablespoons cornstarch
½ teaspoon freshly ground black pepper	1 cup dry white wine
	½ cup chicken broth
6 tablespoons butter	½ cup heavy cream
3 tablespoons cognac	

Wash and dry the chicken pieces; roll in a mixture of the flour, salt, and pepper.

Melt 4 tablespoons butter in a skillet; sauté the chicken until browned on all sides. Transfer chicken to a casserole. Heat the cognac in a ladle; set aflame and pour over the chicken.

Melt the remaining butter in the skillet; sauté the onion and mushrooms 5 minutes. Mix the cornstarch with the wine, then stir into the skillet with the broth. Bring to a boil, stirring constantly. Stir in the cream, then add to the chicken. Cover, and bake in a 350° oven 45 minutes, or until chicken is tender. Taste for seasoning.

Serves 6-8.

Serve with champagne, a dry German white wine, or a rosé.

POULET NIVERNAIS
CHICKEN WITH DUMPLINGS

2 3-pound fryers, disjointed	½ teaspoon marjoram
4 teaspoons salt	1 bay leaf
½ teaspoon freshly ground black pepper	1¼ cups dry white wine
¼ pound butter	½ teaspoon saffron
2 cloves	1 cup sour cream, scalded
12 small white onions	1½ cups sifted flour
1 cup sliced mushrooms	2 teaspoons baking powder
1 clove garlic, minced	2 eggs, beaten
¼ teaspoon thyme	1/3 cup milk
	1 tablespoon minced parsley

Season the chicken with 3 teaspoons of the salt, and the pepper. Melt the butter in a casserole or heavy saucepan; brown the chicken in it. Stick the cloves in an onion and add with all the onions and the mushrooms; cook over low heat 5 minutes. Stir in the garlic, thyme, marjoram, bay leaf, and wine. Cover, and bake in a 375° oven 45 minutes, or until chicken is almost tender. Remove from the oven and place over direct low heat. Stir the saffron and sour cream into the pan; taste for seasoning. While the chicken continues to cook, prepare the dumpling batter.

Sift the flour, baking powder, and remaining salt into a bowl. Beat in the eggs and milk. Drop the mixture by the teaspoon around the edge of the casserole. Cover, and cook 15 minutes without raising the cover. When done, sprinkle with the parsley.

Serves 8-10.

Serve with a dry German white wine, or a *rosé*.

POLLO À LA MANCHEGA
CHICKEN AND VEGETABLE STEW

3½-pound fryer, disjointed	1 cup grated carrots
2 tablespoons butter	3 cups shredded cabbage
2 tablespoons olive oil	2 teaspoons salt
1 cup chopped onion	½ teaspoon freshly ground
2 cloves garlic, minced	black pepper
2 tablespoons chopped	¾ cup dry white wine
parsley	½ cup pitted green olives

Wash and dry the chicken pieces. Heat the butter and oil in a Dutch oven or casserole; brown the chicken in it. Remove chicken. In the fat remaining in the pan, sauté the onion, garlic, and parsley for 10 minutes. Return the chicken and add the carrots, cabbage, salt, and pepper. Cook over low heat 10 minutes. Add the wine and olives. Cover, and cook over low heat 45 minutes, or until the chicken is tender.

Serves 4.

Serve with a white Burgundy, Bordeaux, a dry German white wine, or a *rosé*.

STUFFED BROILERS

2 2½-pound broilers, split	1 cup chopped onion
3 teaspoons salt	½ cup chopped celery and
¾ teaspoon freshly ground	leaves
black pepper	¼ teaspoon thyme
6 slices white bread, trimmed	2 tablespoons minced parsley
¾ pound chicken livers	½ cup dry sherry
6 tablespoons butter	

Wash and dry the chicken halves; season with 2 teaspoons salt and ½ teaspoon pepper. Soak the bread in water, then drain and mash. Chop the raw livers.

Melt 3 tablespoons of the butter in a skillet; sauté the

onion and celery 5 minutes. Mix in the livers, and the remaining salt and pepper; sauté 5 minutes, stirring frequently. Mix in the bread, thyme, and parsley; taste for
seasoning.

Melt the remaining butter in a baking pan. Arrange the
chicken halves in it, skin side up. Bake in a 350° oven 20
minutes. Turn over, skin side down, and fill the cavities
with the stuffing. Pour the sherry over the stuffing and
around the chicken. Bake 20 minutes longer, or until the
chicken is tender.

Serves 4-8.

Serve with a white Burgundy or Bordeaux, a Loire
Valley wine like Pouilly-Fumé, or a dry Italian white wine
like Soave.

PUCHERO DE GALLINA
STUFFED POACHED CHICKEN

5-pound pullet	¼ cup melted butter
3 extra chicken livers	2 eggs, beaten
3 teaspoons salt	2 cups dry white wine
¾ teaspoon freshly ground black pepper	4 cups water
	1 onion
1½ cups dry bread crumbs	1 carrot
1 clove garlic, minced	1 parsnip
2 tablespoons chopped parsley	3 whole cloves garlic
	1 tablespoon olive oil
¼ teaspoon thyme	1 tablespoon flour

Wash and dry the chicken. Reserve the livers. Season
the chicken with 2½ teaspoons of the salt and ½ teaspoon
pepper.

Mix together the bread crumbs, garlic, parsley, thyme,
butter, and remaining salt and pepper; mix in the eggs.
Stuff the chicken, and sew or skewer the opening securely.
Truss the chicken.

Combine the wine, water, onion, carrot, parsnip, and
garlic in a heavy deep pan. Bring to a boil. Add the
chicken; cover, and cook over medium heat 2½ hours, or
until the chicken is tender. Remove the chicken to a hot
platter and keep hot. Reduce the broth to 2½ cups. Strain.

While the chicken is cooking, chop the livers very fine,

then sauté in the oil for 2 minutes. Blend in the flour. Mix a little hot broth with the livers, then combine the mixture with the broth in the pan; cook 5 minutes. Carve the chicken, and pour the sauce over it.

Serves 4-6.

Serve with a white Burgundy or Bordeaux, a dry Italian white wine like Orvieto, or a *rosé*.

BREAST OF CHICKEN AND HAM

3 whole chicken breasts	½ teaspoon sage
¼ cup flour	6 slices prosciutto or
1½ teaspoons salt	cooked ham
¼ teaspoon white pepper	¾ cup dry white wine
4 tablespoons butter	

Have the chicken breasts cut in half through the breastbone. Remove the skin and bones. Place each piece of chicken between 2 sheets of waxed paper and pound very thin. Dip the pounded chicken in a mixture of the flour, salt, and pepper.

Melt the butter in a skillet; sauté the chicken breasts until browned on the under side. Turn chicken over and sprinkle with the sage. Cover with the ham. Sauté 5 minutes. Add the wine; bring to a boil, and cook over low heat 2 minutes. Transfer chicken to a heated serving dish, ham side up. Boil the pan juices for 2 minutes, and stir to break up the glaze. Pour over the chicken.

Serves 6.

Serve with a white Burgundy, an Alsatian wine like Traminer, a dry German white wine, or a *rosé*.

CHICKEN, CHEESE, AND HAM ROLLS

3 whole chicken breasts	6 thin slices Swiss cheese
¼ cup flour	6 cooked asparagus tips
2 teaspoons salt	6 tablespoons butter
¼ teaspoon white pepper	¾ cup Marsala or sweet sherry
6 thin slices cooked ham	

Have the chicken breasts cut in half through the breastbone. Remove the skin and bones. Place each piece of chicken between two pieces of waxed paper and pound as thin as possible. Dip one side of each piece in a mixture of the flour, salt, and pepper. On the undipped side place a slice of ham, then a slice of cheese and a asparagus tip. Roll up carefully and tie with thread or fasten with toothpicks.

Melt 4 tablespoons butter in a skillet; sauté the rolls over very low heat until browned and tender. Transfer to a heated serving dish. To the skillet, add the wine and remaining butter. Bring to a boil, scraping the pan for browned particles. Pour over the rolls.

Serves 6.

Serve with a red Bordeaux or Burgundy, an Italian red wine like Volpolicella, or a *rosé*.

CHICKENBURGER

2 whole chicken breasts	¼ teaspoon nutmeg
1 pound veal	1/3 cup dry sherry
3 slices white bread, trimmed	1 cup light cream
¾ cup milk	4 tablespoons butter
1¼ teaspoons salt	

Remove the skin and bones of the chicken; cut the chicken into strips. Cut the veal into small pieces. Grind the veal and chicken in a meat grinder, using the finest blade.

Soak the bread in the milk, mash and squeeze dry. Mix together the bread, ground meat, salt, nutmeg, sherry, and cream; form into 8-10 flat patties.

Melt the butter in a skillet; sauté the patties in it 10 minutes on each side, or until browned on both sides. Serve with a mushroom or cream sauce, if desired.

Serves 4-5.

POULET FINANCIÈRE
CHICKEN WITH CHICKEN LIVERS AND OLIVES

4-pound pullet, disjointed	½ cup chicken broth
1½ teaspoons salt	1 cup dry red wine
½ teaspoon freshly ground black pepper	½ pound chicken livers, cut in halves
1/3 cup flour	4 tablespoons butter
2 tablespoons olive oil	1 tablespoon flour
¼ pound mushrooms, sliced	½ cup pitted green olives

Wash and dry the chicken pieces; roll in a mixture of the salt, pepper, and flour. Heat the oil in a casserole; brown the chicken in it. Add the mushrooms, chicken broth, and wine. Cover, and cook over low heat 25 minutes. Sauté the livers in 2 tablespoons of the butter. Knead the flour with the remaining butter; add to the gravy in small bits, then add the olives and sautéed livers; cook 10 minutes longer, or until chicken is tender. Taste for seasoning.

Serves 6-8.

Serve with a light red Bordeaux or Burgundy, an Italian red wine like Valpolicella, or a *rosé*.

SPEZZATO DI POLLO
CHICKEN AND LIVERS IN WHITE WINE

2 2½-pound fryers	or green onions
3 tablespoons olive oil	¾ cup diced mushrooms
4 tablespoons butter	1½ cups dry white wine
2½ teaspoons salt	½ cup chicken broth
¾ teaspoon freshly ground black pepper	½ pound chicken livers, cut in half
1 clove garlic, minced	2 tablespoons minced parsley
2 tablespoons chopped chives	

Have the chicken chopped up, bone and all, in small pieces. Wash and dry thoroughly. Heat the oil and 1 tablespoon of the butter in a deep skillet; sauté the chicken in it until browned. Mix in 2 teaspoons of the salt, ½ teaspoon pepper, the garlic, chives, mushrooms, wine, and broth. Bring to a boil, and cook over medium heat 30 minutes, or until chicken is tender.

Melt the remaining butter in a separate skillet; sauté the livers in it 5 minutes, or until very little pink remains. Season with the remaining salt and pepper. Add to the chicken; cook 5 minutes longer. Sprinkle with the parsley.

Serves 6-8.

Serve with a dry Italian white wine like Orvieto, a dry white Burgundy or Bordeaux, or a *rosé*.

RICE WITH CHICKEN LIVERS AND MUSHROOM SAUCE

6 tablespoons butter
¾ cup finely chopped onion
2 cups raw rice
¾ cup Marsala or sweet sherry
5 cups hot chicken broth
1½ teaspoons salt
½ cup thinly sliced onion
½ cup julienne-cut prosciutto ham

¼ pound chicken livers, diced
½ pound mushrooms, sliced
½ cup beef broth
¼ teaspoon freshly ground black pepper
1 bay leaf
¼ teaspoon thyme

Melt half the butter in a saucepan; sauté the chopped onion until yellow and transparent. Stir in the rice until lightly browned. Add ¼ cup wine; cook until wine is absorbed. Add 2 cups of the chicken broth and half the salt; cover, and cook over low heat 25 minutes, adding the remaining chicken broth as it becomes absorbed by the rice. Meanwhile prepare the sauce.

Melt the remaining butter in a small saucepan; sauté the sliced onion and ham 5 minutes. Add the livers and mushrooms; sauté 5 minutes, stirring frequently. Mix in the beef broth, pepper, bay leaf, thyme, and the remaining wine and salt. Cook over low heat 10 minutes. Taste for seasoning, and discard the bay leaf. Mix half the sauce with the rice. Heap in a bowl and pour remaining sauce over the top.

Serves 4-6.

Serve with a light red Bordeaux or Burgundy.

GALLINA CON ARROZ
CHICKEN IN RICE RING

2 3-pound fryers, disjointed
3 tablespoons olive oil
1 cup minced onion
¾ cup chopped green peppers
2 cloves garlic, minced
1 tablespoon minced parsley
1 8-ounce can tomato sauce
2 cups dry white wine
1 cup boiling water

2½ teaspoons salt
¼ teaspoon dried ground red peppers
½ cup seedless raisins
4 cups cooked, drained rice
4 tablespoons melted butter
2 cups grated Cheddar cheese
4 eggs, beaten
1 cup sliced toasted almonds

Wash and dry the chicken pieces.

Heat the oil in a Dutch oven or heavy saucepan; sauté the onion and green peppers 5 minutes. Add the garlic, parsley, and chicken; sauté 15 minutes, turning the chicken to brown all sides. Mix in the tomato sauce, wine, water, salt, and ground red peppers. Cover, and cook over low heat for 1 hour, or until chicken is tender. Cut the chicken from the bones and return to the sauce. Add the raisins; cook over low heat 15 minutes. Taste for seasoning.

Mix together the rice, butter, cheese, and eggs. Pack into a 9-inch buttered ring mold. Bake in a 350° oven 20 minutes or until set. Run a knife around the edges and carefully turn out onto a hot platter. Put the chicken mixture in the center and sprinkle with the almonds.

Serves 6-8.

Serve with a dry German white wine, a white Burgundy, an Alsatian wine like Traminer, or a *rosé*.

SQUABS WITH PEAS

4 squabs	¼ pound ham, julienne-cut
1 tablespoon salt	1 cup dry white wine
¾ teaspoon freshly ground black pepper	½ cup chicken broth
½ teaspoon thyme	1 pound green peas, shelled, or 1 package frozen peas, thawed
4 tablespoons butter	
1½ cups chopped onion	

Wash and dry the squabs; rub inside and out with a mixture of the salt, pepper, and thyme. Melt the butter in a Dutch oven or heavy deep skillet; sauté the chopped onion 10 minutes. Add the squabs; brown on all sides. Mix in the ham and half the wine; cook over medium heat 10 minutes. Mix in the broth and remaining wine; cover, and cook over low heat 30 minutes. Add the peas; re-cover, and cook 15 minutes. Taste for seasoning. Transfer the squabs to a serving dish and pour gravy over all.

Serves 4.

Serve with a white Burgundy, a dry German white wine, or a *rosé*.

STUFFED SQUABS

1 cup wild rice, washed and drained	black pepper
3 cups chicken broth	6 squabs or Rock Cornish hens
¼ pound butter	1 tablespoon salt
1 cup chopped onion	1 teaspoon paprika
¼ pound mushrooms, chopped	12 small white onions
1 teaspoon Worcestershire sauce	1 cup dry white wine
¾ teaspoon freshly ground	¼ cup cognac

Combine the wild rice and broth in a saucepan. Cover, bring to a boil, and cook over low heat 25 minutes, or until rice is tender and dry. Melt 4 tablespoons butter in a skillet; sauté the chopped onion and mushrooms 10 minutes. Add to the rice, with the Worcestershire sauce and ¼ teaspoon pepper. Mix lightly and taste for seasoning.

Season the birds with the salt, paprika, and remaining pepper; stuff, and sew or skewer openings.

Melt the remaining butter in a shallow roasting pan. Brown the birds and whole onions. Add the wine; bake in a 375° oven 40 minutes, or until birds are tender, basting frequently. Remove from oven and pour warmed cognac over the birds. Set aflame, and serve when flames die.

Serves 6.

Serve with a white Burgundy, a dry German white wine, or a *rosé*.

SQUABS IN RED WINE

4 1-pound squabs	2 tablespoons olive oil
2 teaspoons salt	1½ cups sliced onion
½ teaspoon freshly ground black pepper	2 cloves garlic, minced
4 slices bacon	2 carrots, sliced
	2 cups dry red wine

Wash, clean, and dry the squabs. Rub with the salt and pepper. Cut the livers and gizzards in small pieces. Wrap a slice of bacon around each squab and fasten with a toothpick.

Heat the oil in a Dutch oven. Add the squabs, onion slices, garlic and carrots. Cook until squabs are browned

on all sides. Add the livers and giblets and wine. Bring to
a boil, cover, and cook over low heat 1 hour, or until the
squabs are tender. If gravy is too thin, thicken with 1 tablespoon flour kneaded with 1 tablespoon butter.

Serves 4.

Serve with a red Bordeaux wine, a Beaujolais, or any
rosé.

CORNISH HEN IN CHERRY SAUCE

2 Rock Cornish hens	3 tablespoons sugar
2 teaspoons salt	1 cup port wine
½ teaspoon freshly ground black pepper	2 teaspoons cornstarch
¼ pound (1 stick) butter	1½ cups canned pitted black cherries
3 tablespoons wine vinegar	

Season the hens with the salt and pepper. Melt half the
butter in a shallow baking pan, and pour into the hens.
Bake in a 375° oven 50 minutes, or until birds are browned
and tender, basting frequently. Cut birds in half, arrange
in a serving platter, and keep warm while making sauce.

Cook the vinegar and sugar until caramel-colored. Add
the port wine to the pan juices and reduce to half over
high heat, scraping up the glaze from the pan. Stir in the
caramel. Mix the cornstarch with 2 tablespoons cold water
and stir into the pan, cooking until thickened. Mix in the
cherries and the remaining butter, and cook over low heat
5 minutes. Pour sauce over birds and serve, accompanied
by wild rice.

Serves 2-4.

Serve with a red Burgundy or Bordeaux, or if you wish,
with a red Rhône wine like Hermitage or Châteauneuf-du-
Pape.

ROCK CORNISH HEN IN CAPER SAUCE

2 Rock Cornish hens, halved	1 tablespoon flour
1½ teaspoons salt	¾ cup dry white wine
½ teaspoon freshly ground black pepper	4 anchovy fillets, mashed
3 tablespoons butter	2 tablespoons drained capers
	2 tablespoons lemon juice

Wash and dry the hens. Season with the salt and pepper. Melt half the butter in a deep skillet. Brown the birds in it very well. Blend in the flour until browned. Add the wine, anchovies, capers, and lemon juice. Cover, and cook over low heat 30 minutes, or until birds are tender. Add the remaining butter.

Serves 2-4.

Serve with a white Burgundy, a dry German white wine, or a white Rhône wine like Châteauneuf-du-Pape Blanc, or a *rosé*.

CHAPON SAUTÉ À LA BORDELAISE
CAPON, BORDEAUX STYLE

¼ pound butter	thinly sliced
3 tablespoons olive o.	3 large onions, thinly sliced
5-pound capon, disjoi... .d	½ cup milk
2 teaspoons salt	½ cup flour
½ teaspoon freshly ground black pepper	Vegetable oil for deep frying
	1 clove garlic, minced
1 package frozen artichokes, thawed	1 cup dry white wine
	1 teaspoon meat glaze
3 potatoes, peeled and very	1 tablespoon tomato paste

Heat 2 tablespoons butter and the oil in a heavy sauce-pan; sauté the capon in it until browned on all sides. Season with the salt and pepper. Cover, and cook over low heat 45 minutes, or until the capon is tender. Transfer to a hot serving platter and keep warm.

While chicken is cooking, sauté the artichokes in 3 table-spoons butter for 5 minutes, turning them frequently. Sprinkle with salt. Dry potato slices thoroughly, and sauté in the remaining butter until golden brown on both sides. Sprinkle with salt.

Separate the onion slices into rings. Dip in the milk and then in the flour, and fry in 375° oil until crisp and golden.

Add the garlic to butter remaining in pan in which capon was cooked. Sauté 2 minutes. Add wine, meat glaze, and tomato paste and stir to scrape any browned particles from pan. Cook over low heat 5 minutes.

Arrange the artichokes, potato slices and onion rings around the capon. Pour sauce over capon and serve.

Serves 4-6.

Serve with a white Burgundy, a dry German white wine, a white Rhône wine like Hermitage Blanc, or a *rosé*.

CHAPON LUCULLUS
CAPON IN WINE SAUCE

2 pair sweetbreads
6 tablespoons butter
5-pound capon, disjointed
1 cup sliced onion
½ cup sliced carrot
2 teaspoons salt
½ teaspoon freshly ground

black pepper
1 cup sliced mushrooms
½ cup diced ham
1 cup dry white wine
¼ cup cognac
¾ cup heavy cream

Soak the sweetbreads for 2 hours in cold water to cover. Drain. Cook in lightly salted water 10 minutes. Drain, cool, remove membranes, and dice. Refrigerate while preparing the capon.

Melt half the butter in a casserole. Add the capon pieces, sliced onion, carrots, salt, and pepper. Cover, and cook over low heat 45 minutes, turning the pieces frequently. Add the remaining butter, the mushrooms, ham, sweetbreads, and wine. Cook 20 minutes. Mix in the cognac and cream. Cook 5 minutes. Taste for seasoning.

Serves 6-8.

Serve with a white Burgundy, a Loire Valley wine like Sancerre, a dry Italian white wine like Soave, or a *rosé*.

MARINATED STUFFED TURKEY

12-pound turkey
3 cups dry red wine
2½ cups chopped onion
2 cloves garlic, minced
5 teaspoons salt
1 teaspoon freshly ground
    black pepper
1 bay leaf
1/3 cup olive oil

¾ cup chopped green peppers
½ pound ground pork
2 cups ground almonds
3 hard-cooked eggs
1¼ cups seedless raisins
1 cup sliced pimiento-
    stuffed green olives
½ teaspoon marjoram
1½ cups finely diced bread

Wash, clean, and dry the turkey.

In a glass or pottery bowl, combine the wine, 1 cup of the chopped onion, the garlic, 3 teaspoons salt, the pepper, and bay leaf. Marinate the turkey in the mixture in the refrigerator overnight. Turn and baste turkey a few times.

Heat the oil in a skillet; sauté the green peppers and remaining onion 5 minutes. Add the pork, and cook until browned and no pink remains. Season with the remaining salt and mix in the almonds, eggs, raisins, olives, marjoram, and bread. Taste for seasoning. Drain the turky, stuff, and close the openings with skewers or thread. Place in a roasting pan; roast in a 325° oven for 3½ hours, adding the marinade after 1 hour. Baste frequently until turkey is tender.

Serves 10-14.

Serve with a light red Burgundy, especially a Beaujolais, or a Rhône wine like Côte-Rôtie, or a dry Italian red wine like Barolo.

CANARD AU GRAND MARNIER
DUCK WITH GRAND MARNIER

5-pound duck	3 tablespoons wine vinegar
2½ teaspoons salt	¾ cup orange juice
1 orange, cut in half	½ cup Grand Marnier
1½ cups dry white wine	3 tablespoons grated orange
½ cup sugar	rind

Clean the duck, wash, and dry. Rub the salt into the skin and cavity; put the orange in the cavity. Place the duck on a rack in a shallow roasting pan. Roast in a 425° oven 45 minutes, turning the duck to brown all sides. Pour off the fat, remove the rack, and add the wine. Reduce heat to 350°, and roast 1¼ hours longer or until the duck is tender. Baste occasionally.

While the duck is roasting, prepare the sauce. Combine the sugar and vingear in a heavy saucepan; cook over medium heat until caramel-colored. Stir in the orange juice, Grand Marnier, and orange rind. Cook over low heat 5 minutes. Skim the fat from the pan juices and add juices to the sauce. Taste for seasoning.

Carve the duck and pour sauce over it. If desired,

warmed cognac may be set aflame on the duck just before serving.

Serves 4.

Serve with a red or white Burgundy, or a *rosé*.

CANARD AU VIN ROUGE
DUCK IN RED WINE

5-pound duck
2 teaspoons salt
½ teaspoon freshly ground pepper
3 tablespoons butter
3 tablespoons flour
1 cup chicken stock
1 cup dry red wine
1 tablespoon chopped onion
1 teaspoon chopped parsley
2 teaspoons grated orange rind
¼ teaspoon rosemary
1 bay leaf

Wash the duck, dry, and season with the salt and pepper. Chop the liver and refrigerate. Place the duck on a rack in a shallow pan; roast in a 375° oven 1½ hours, turning the duck to brown all sides. Carve the duck into serving-size pieces, removing as many bones as possible.

Melt the butter in a saucepan; mix in the flour until browned. Add stock and wine, stirring steadily to the boiling point. Add the carved duck, the onion, parsley, orange rind, rosemary, and bay leaf. Cook over low heat 1 hour. Discard the bay leaf. Stir the chopped liver into the sauce; cook 5 minutes. Serve on rounds of toasted bread.

Serves 4-5.

Serve with a red Bordeaux or Burgundy, or a *rosé*.

DUCK AND VEGETABLES IN RED WINE

5-pound duck, disjointed
1 tablespoon vegetable oil
12 small white onions
1 carrot, sliced
1 clove garlic, minced
2 teaspoons salt
½ teaspoon freshly ground black pepper
2 cups dry red wine
½ cup chicken broth
½ pound mushrooms, sliced
2 cups cubed sweet potatoes

Wash the duck pieces, remove as much fat as possible, and dry. Heat the oil in a casserole; brown the duck in it on all sides. Pour off the fat. Add the onions, carrot, garlic, salt, and pepper; cook until onions turn golden. Pour off the fat again. Add the wine and broth. Cover, and cook over low heat 45 minutes. Skim the fat, then add the mushrooms and potatoes. Cook 25 minutes longer. Taste for seasoning.

Serves 4.

Serve with a red Burgundy, a Rhône wine like Hermitage, or an Italian red wine like Barolo.

CANARD AUX OLIVES
DUCK WITH OLIVES

5-pound duck	½ teaspoon thyme
2 teaspoons salt	1 bay leaf
½ teaspoon freshly ground black pepper	1 tablespoon flour
1 teaspoon paprika	¾ cup chicken broth
1 cup dry white wine	1½ cups sliced stuffed olives

Clean the duck, removing as much fat as possible. Season with the salt, pepper, and paprika. Place on a rack in a shallow roasting pan. Roast in a 425° oven 45 minutes, turning the duck to brown all sides. Pour off the fat, remove the rack, and add the wine, thyme, and bay leaf. Reduce heat to 350°, and roast duck 1 hour longer, or until tender, basting frequently.

Transfer the duck to a platter; place pan over direct low heat. Mix the flour with the broth and add to the pan juices, stirring steadily to the boiling point. Add the olives. Cook over low heat 5 minutes. Taste for seasoning. Carve the duck and pour the sauce over it.

Serves 4.

Serve with a red Burgundy, or a Rhône wine like Châteauneuf-du-Pape.

BRAISED DUCK WITH OLIVE SAUCE

5-6 pound duck, disjointed	½ cup diced celery
2 teaspoons salt	1 cup dry red wine
½ teaspoon black pepper	½ cup beef broth
½ teaspoon oregano	1 bay leaf
¾ cup chopped onion	1 cup sliced black olives

Wash the duck, remove as much fat as possible, and dry. Rub the pieces with a mixture of the salt, pepper, and oregano. In a Dutch oven or heavy casserole, brown the duck pieces on all sides. Pour off the fat. Add the chopped onion and the celery; cook 10 minutes. Pour off the fat again. Add the wine, broth, and bay leaf; bring to a boil, cover, and cook over low heat 1 hour, or until tender. Turn pieces and baste frequently. Arrange the duck on a heated serving dish and keep warm.

Skim the fat off the gravy and discard the bay leaf. Add the olives; cook 5 minutes. Taste for seasoning. Pour the sauce over the duck.

Serves 4.

Serve with a dry red Bordeaux or Burgundy.

DUCKLING WITH SOUR RED CHERRIES

5-pound duck	½ cup sweet sherry
2 teaspoons salt	2 tablespoons butter
½ teaspoon freshly ground black pepper	2 tablespoons flour
¼ teaspoon marjoram	2 cups canned, pitted sour red cherries
2 cups chicken broth	

Wash and dry the duck; rub inside and out with salt, pepper, and marjoram. Combine in a heavy saucepan with the chicken broth. Cover, and cook over low heat for 1 hour, or until duck is tender.

Add the sherry. Cook over high heat 5 minutes. Remove the duck from the gravy, then remove the skin. Carve into serving-size pieces. Place on a hot serving platter and keep hot in the oven. Skim the fat off the gravy.

Knead together the flour and butter. Add to the gravy in small bits, stirring constantly until gravy is thickened. Add the cherries to gravy and pour over the duck. Serve very hot.

Serves 4.

Serve with a red Burgundy wine.

CANARD VÉRONIQUE
BRAISED DUCK WITH GRAPES

5-pound duck, disjointed	2 tablespoons butter
1½ teaspoons salt	1 cup port wine
¼ teaspoon freshly ground	2 tablespoons currant jelly
black pepper	1 cup seedless grapes,
¼ teaspoon nutmeg	cut in half

Wash and dry the duck pieces; remove as much fat as possible, then rub with the salt, pepper, and nutmeg.

Melt the butter in a casserole; brown the duck in it. Pour off the fat, and add the port and jelly. Bring to a boil, cover, and cook over low heat 45 minutes, or until duck is tender. Skim off the fat, and add the grapes; cook 5 minutes longer.

Serves 4.

Serve with a red Burgundy wine.

ROAST LONG ISLAND DUCK

2 5-pound ducks	1 cup dry sherry
3 teaspoons salt	2 tablespoons cornstarch
½ teaspoon pepper	1 cup water
1 cup sugar	3 tablespoons julienne-cut
2 cups currant jelly	orange rind
1½ cups orange juice	

Clean the ducks, and remove as much fat as possible. Season with the salt and pepper. Place on a rack in a roasting pan; roast in a 400° oven 1¼ hours, basting frequently. Reduce heat to 350° and roast 1 hour longer, or until the ducks are tender, crisp, and brown.

In a saucepan, combine the sugar, currant jelly, and orange juice. Bring to a boil, and cook over low heat 15 minutes. Stir in the sherry, and cook 5 minutes longer. Mix the cornstarch with the water and add to the saucepan, stirring constantly to the boiling point. Add the rind.

Carve the duck in quarters, and pour the sauce over it. Garnish with a slice of orange and a maraschino cherry.

Serves 6-8.

ANITRA ARROSTITA
ROAST STUFFED DUCK

5-6 pound duck
2 teaspoons salt
½ teaspoon freshly ground
    black pepper
2 cloves garlic, minced
2 tablespoons olive oil
¾ cup minced onion
1 pound sausage meat

3 slices toast, diced
⅛ teaspoon crushed dried
    red peppers
½ teaspoon rosemary
½ cup chopped black olives
¾ cup Marsala wine or
    sweet sherry

Wash and dry the duck; rub inside and out with the salt, pepper, and garlic.

Heat the oil in a skillet; sauté the onion 5 minutes. Add the sausage meat; let brown, stirring frequently. Pour off the fat. Mix in the diced toast, red peppers, rosemary, and olives. Cool 15 minutes. Stuff the duck. Close the opening with skewers, or sew it. Place on a rack in a roasting pan. Roast in a 425° oven 30 minutes. Pour off the fat. Reduce heat to 350°. Roast 30 minutes. Pour off the fat. Remove the rack. Add the wine; roast 1½ hours longer, or until duck is tender, basting frequently.

Serves 4-5.

Serve with a dry red Bordeaux or Burgundy.

DUCK CASSEROLE

5-pound duck, disjointed
1½ teaspoons salt
½ teaspoon freshly ground
    black pepper
2 tablespoons vegetable oil
¾ cup chopped onion
1 cup chopped green peppers
1 clove garlic, minced
½ cup canned tomato sauce

1 cup dry sherry
1 bay leaf
1 cup cooked or canned
    green peas
½ pound mushrooms, sliced
    and sautéed
½ cup sliced pimiento-
    stuffed olives

Wash and dry the duck; remove as much fat as possible. Rub the pieces with the salt and pepper.

Heat the oil in a skillet; brown the duck pieces in it. Drain and transfer to a casserole. In the fat remaining, sauté the chopped onion, green pepper, and garlic 10 minutes. Drain off the fat, and add the vegetables to the casserole with the tomato sauce, sherry, and bay leaf. Cover and bake in a 350° oven 1 hour, or until duck is tender. Skim off the fat, discard the bay leaf, and add the peas, mushrooms, and olives. Bake 5 minutes longer.

Serves 4.

Serve with a red Burgundy wine.

Meat

ENTRECÔTE GRILLÉ CHAROLLAIS BOURGUIGNONNE
GRILLED STEAK, BURGUNDY STYLE

2 tablespoons butter
2 tablespoons finely chopped
    shallots or onion
½ teaspoon flour
1 cup dry red wine
1 clove garlic, minced

1 tablespoon tomato paste
1 tablespoon Madeira or
    sweet sherry
1 shell or club steak, cut
    2 inches thick

Melt the butter in a skillet and sauté the shallots until soft but not brown. Blend in the flour. Add the wine, stirring constantly to the boiling point. Mix in the garlic, tomato paste, and Madeira. Cook over low heat 30 minutes.

Broil the steak in a hot broiler to desired degree of rareness. Serve with the red wine sauce.

Serves 2.

Serve with a red Burgundy or Bordeaux, a red Rhône wine like Châteauneuf-du-Pape, or an Italian red wine like Barolo.

STEAK AU POIVRE
PEPPER STEAK

1 tablespoon black pepper-
    corns
2 boneless club or shell steaks,
    cut 1 inch thick
1 tablespoon olive oil
2 tablespoons sweet butter
1 tablespoon chopped shallots

    or onion
1 cup dry red wine
1 teaspoon prepared French
    mustard
1 teaspoon Worcestershire
    sauce

Crush the peppercorns coarsely. (Put them in a towel and pound with a hammer, or use a mortar and pestle, or put through a coarse peppermill.) With the heel of the hand, press the crushed peppercorns well into both sides of the steaks.

Heat the oil in a skillet; quickly brown the steaks in it on both sides. While the steaks are browning, melt 1 tablespoon butter in another skillet; sauté the chopped shallots 2 minutes. Then add the steaks, and cook 2 minutes on each side. Remove the steaks to a heated platter and keep hot. Add the wine to the shallots; cook over high heat until reduced to ¼ the original quantity. Remove from the heat and immediately stir in the mustard, Worcestershire sauce, and the remaining butter, broken into small pieces. Pour over the steaks.

Serves 2-4.

Serve with a red Burgundy or Bordeaux, or any dry Italian red wine.

BOEUF RÔTI À LA BORDELAISE
ROAST BEEF, BORDEAUX STYLE

3-pound rump roast of beef	½ cup olive oil
1 onion, sliced	1 cup dry white wine
2 shallots, chopped	2 teaspoons salt
4 sprigs parsley	½ teaspoon freshly ground
1 bay leaf	black pepper
½ teaspoon thyme	1 tablespoon wine vinegar

Trim the fat from meat and reserve. Marinate the meat overnight in a mixture of the sliced onion, shallots, parsley, bay leaf, thyme, oil, wine, salt, and pepper.

Put a strip of the reserved beef fat in the bottom of a roasting pan. Strain the marinade and spread the vegetables and herbs on the fat. Put meat on top and season with salt and pepper; place another piece of fat over it and add ¼ cup marinade. Roast in a 350° oven 1¼ hours, basting often. Transfer meat to a serving platter and keep hot.

Strain juices from roasting pan; skim off the fat, and combine the juice in a saucepan with the remaining strained marinade. Cook over high heat 10 minutes. Add wine vinegar, reheat, and serve separately as a sauce for roast.

Serves 6-8.

Serve with any dry red Bordeaux or Burgundy.

CARNE ASADO
MARINATED ROAST BEEF

6-pound rolled roast of beef	2 cups chopped onion
2 teaspoons salt	1 cup chopped green peppers
1 teaspoon freshly ground	2 cups peeled diced tomatoes
black pepper	1 bay leaf
1 teaspoon Spanish paprika	1 cup sliced sautéed
3 cloves garlic, minced	mushrooms
1½ cups dry red wine	1 8-ounce can green peas,
½ cup wine vinegar	drained
¼ cup olive oil	

Rub the meat with a mixture of the salt, pepper, paprika, and garlic. Marinate the meat in a mixture of the wine and vinegar in the refrigerator 24 hours, turning the meat and basting a few times. Remove from refrigerator 2 hours before roasting.

Drain the meat, reserving the marinade. Heat the oil in a roasting pan over direct heat; brown the meat in it on all sides. Pour off half the fat. Add the chopped onion, green peppers, tomatoes, bay leaf, and half the marinade. Insert a meat thermometer in the center of the meat and roast in a 350° oven to desired degree of rareness, basting frequently (or without thermometer about 13 minutes per pound for rare, 15 for medium, or 18 for well done). Add remaining marinade from time to time. Transfer meat to a hot platter. Discard bay leaf, skim the fat off and purée gravy in a blender, or force through a sieve. Taste for seasoning. If too thick, add a little water. Add the mushrooms and green peas; heat, and serve in a sauceboat.

Serves 8-10.

Serve with a red Bordeaux or Burgundy, especially a Beaujolais, or an Italian red wine like Chianti, or a Rhône wine like Châteauneuf-du-Pape.

RIB ROAST IN WINE

5-pound rolled rib roast
¼ cup flour
4 tablespoons butter
1 cup chopped onion
½ cup chopped carrot
1 clove garlic, minced

2 tablespoons warm cognac
2 cups dry red wine
2 teaspoons salt
8 crushed peppercorns
1 bay leaf
½ teaspoon marjoram

Rub the meat with the flour. Heat the butter in a Dutch oven or heavy casserole; brown the meat in it on all sides. Add the chopped onion, carrot, and garlic, and cook until browned. Add the cognac and set aflame. When flames die down, add the wine, salt, peppercorns, bay leaf, and marjoram. Cover, and bake in a 325° oven about 3 hours, or until meat is tender.

Transfer the meat to a hot platter. Taste the gravy for seasoning, strain, and serve in a gravy boat.

Serves 8-10.

Serve with any dry red Burgundy or Bordeaux.

COSTA DI MANZO AL VINO ROSSO
MARINATED ROAST BEEF, ITALIAN STYLE

3-rib roast
3 cups dry red wine
¾ cup sliced onion
½ cup sliced carrot
2 cloves garlic, minced

2 bay leaves
½ teaspoon freshly ground
    black pepper
2½ teaspoons salt

Marinate the meat in a mixture of the wine, onion, carrot, garlic, bay leaves, and pepper for 24 hours in the refrigerator, basting and turning the meat several times.

Drain, reserving the marinade. Dry the meat with paper towels; rub with the salt. Place in a shallow roasting pan; roast in a 450° oven 20 minutes. Meanwhile, cook the marinade until reduced to half; pour over the meat. Roast a total of 15 minutes a pound, basting frequently. Skim the fat from the gravy, and serve gravy in a sauceboat.

Serves 4-6.

Serve with a red Bordeaux or Burgundy, a Rhône wine like Châteauneuf-du-Pape, or a dry Italian red wine like Barolo.

FILLET OF BEEF IN VERMOUTH

2 tablespoons butter	1 tablespoon flour
4 fillets of beef, cut	¼ cup dry vermouth
1 inch thick	½ cup heavy cream
¾ teaspoon salt	2 tablespoons chopped
¼ teaspoon freshly ground	parsley
black pepper	

Melt the butter in a skillet; brown the fillets in it over high heat, 2 minutes on each side, shaking the pan a few times. Sprinkle the meat with the salt and pepper, and stir the flour into the pan juices; add the vermouth and cream. Cook over medium heat 4 minutes longer, or to desired degree of rareness; turn the fillets once.

Arrange the fillets on a hot serving dish and pour the sauce over them. Sprinkle with the parsley.

Serves 4.

Serve with a red Rhône wine like Châteauneuf-du-Pape, or a dry Italian red wine like Valpolicella or Bardolino.

FILET MIGNON AU PORTO
FILET OF BEEF IN PORT

3 tablespoons butter	½ cup port
4 fillets of beef, cut	½ cup sliced sautéed
1 inch thick	mushrooms
1 teaspoon salt	3 tablespoons heavy cream
¼ teaspoon freshly ground	
black pepper	

Melt the butter in a skillet; brown the fillets in it over high heat 3 minutes on each side, or to desired degree of rareness. Season with the salt and pepper and transfer to a heated serving dish; keep hot.

Stir the port, mushrooms, and cream into the pan juices; cook over low heat 3 minutes. Pour over the fillets.

Serves 4.

Serve with a dry red Burgundy or Bordeaux.

BOEUF AU MADÈRE
BEEF IN MADEIRA

3 pounds eye round of beef	1 pound mushrooms, sliced
2 teaspoons salt	2 teaspoons finely chopped
¼ teaspoon freshly ground	bay leaf
black pepper	¼ cup minced parsley
2 cloves garlic, minced	¼ pound cooked ham,
3 slices bacon, half cooked	chopped
2 cups thinly sliced onions	1½ cups Madeira wine
12 small carrots, scraped	¼ cup cognac

Cut the beef in 1-inch slices; trim off all the fat. Rub meat with a mixture of the salt, pepper, and garlic. Arrange the sliced bacon on the bottom of a heavy deep casserole. Spread ⅓ the sliced onion, carrots, mushrooms, bay leaves, parsley, and chopped ham over the bacon. Arrange 4 slices of beef over it, then repeat the layers twice more. Add the Madeira. Heat the cognac in a ladle, set aflame, and pour into the casserole. When flames die, cover, bring to a boil, and cook over low heat 2½ hours. Shake casserole occasionally.

Serves 6-8.

Serve with a red Bordeaux or Burgundy, a Rhône wine like Hermitage, or an Italian red wine like Barolo.

FILETTO SICILIANA
SAUTÉED FILLET OF BEEF IN MARSALA

3 tablespoons butter	½ teaspoon freshly ground
1 tablespoon olive oil	black pepper
¾ cup sliced onion	1/3 cup Marsala or sherry
4 fillets of beef, cut	¼ cup water
1 inch thick	1 tablespoon minced parsley
1¼ teaspoons salt	

Heat 2 tablespoons butter and the oil in a skillet; sauté the onion slices 10 minutes, then remove. In the fat remaining, cook the fillets over high heat 2 minutes on each side. Stir in the remaining butter, the salt, pepper, wine, water, parsley, and sautéed onion slices. Cook 4 minutes longer, or to desired degree of rareness. Turn the meat once.

Serves 4.

Serve with a dry red Bordeaux or Burgundy, or a dry Italian red wine.

ITALIAN BEEF IN WHITE WINE

4 pounds chuck or rump of beef
2½ teaspoons salt
½ teaspoon freshly ground black pepper
1 clove garlic, minced
2 tablespoons butter
1 cup thinly sliced onion
½ cup sliced carrot
¼ cup wine vinegar
1½ cups dry white wine
1½ pounds tomatoes, peeled and chopped
2 bay leaves
¼ teaspoon sugar
¼ cup heavy cream

Rub the meat with the salt, pepper, and garlic. Melt the butter in a Dutch oven or heavy saucepan; add the meat, sliced onion, and carrot. Cook over medium heat until meat is browned on all sides. Add the vinegar, wine, tomatoes, bay leaves, and sugar. Cover, and cook over low heat 2½ hours, or until meat is tender. Taste for seasoning.

Pour off the gravy, and discard the bay leaves. Purée the gravy in a blender, or force through a sieve. If too thin, cook over high heat a few minutes. Stir in the cream. Slice the beef, and pour gravy over it.

Serves 6-8.

Serve with a dry Italian red wine like Chianti or Bardolino, a Beaujolais, or a red Rhône wine like Côte-Rôtie.

FILETTO AL PÂTÉ
FILLET OF BEEF WITH PÂTÉ

6 fillets of beef, cut 1½ inches thick
1½ teaspoons salt
½ teaspoon freshly ground black pepper
2 tablespoons olive oil
2 tablespoons butter
¼ cup Marsala or sweet sherry
4-ounce can *pâté de foie gras*
¼ cup warmed cognac

Season the fillets with the salt and pepper, and rub with the oil. Let stand at room temperature 1 hour.

Melt the butter in a skillet; cook the fillets over high heat 1 minute on each side, or until browned. Remove. Stir the wine and *pâté* into the pan juices, stirring until smooth. Return the fillets; cook 2 minutes. Pour the cognac over them and set aflame; shake the pan until flames die. Transfer steaks to a serving dish, and pour the sauce over them.

Serves 6.

Serve with a red Bordeaux or Burgundy, a red Rhône wine like Hermitage, or a dry Italian red wine like Valpolicella.

FILET DE BOEUF FARCI
STUFFED FILLET OF BEEF

3-pound fillet of beef	¼ cup chopped cooked ham
2½ teaspoons salt	3 tablespoons minced parsley
¾ teaspoon freshly ground black pepper	⅛ teaspoon thyme
4 truffles, quartered	⅛ teaspoon finely chopped bay leaf
1 cup Madeira or sweet sherry	4-ounce can *pâté de foie gras*
6 tablespoons butter	1 tablespoon cognac
¾ cup chopped onion	1 tablespoon vegetable oil
¾ cup chopped carrot	2 cups beef broth
½ cup chopped celery	1 tablespoon cornstarch

The fillet should weigh 3 pounds after it is trimmed. Do not have any fat wrapped around it, but ask the butcher for a piece of beef suet or pork fat the length of the beef and about 2 inches wide. Cut a deep slit lengthwise on the least attractive side, leaving both ends intact. Season the slit with a little of the salt and pepper.

Marinate the truffles in ⅓ cup of the Madeira for 30 minutes, with cup covered.

Melt 3 tablespoons of the butter in a small saucepan; add the chopped onion, carrot, celery, ham, parsley, thyme, bay leaf, ½ teaspoon of the salt, and ⅛ teaspoon pepper. Cover, and cook over low heat 10 minutes, but do not let brown. Add ⅓ cup of the Madeira; cook over high heat until wine is almost evaporated.

Mash the *pâté*, and beat in the cognac and 1 tablespoon of remaining wine. Spread in the slit of the fillet. Drain the truffles (reserve marinade) and arrange in a row on the *pâté* mixture. Close the slit and cover with the fat; tie securely with thread at close intervals.

In a casserole or heavy pan, heat the oil and 2 tablespoons of the butter. Brown the fillet in it lightly on all sides. Pour off the fat. Sprinkle with the remaining salt and pepper. Spread the cooked vegetables over the meat and add the broth. Bring to a boil, cover, and bake in a 350° oven 40 minutes (rare) or to desired degree of rareness. Baste a few times. Remove the meat, cut the thread, and discard the fat. Place slit side down on a hot serving platter.

Pour the pan juices into a saucepan. Skim off the fat. Add the truffle marinade. Cook over high heat 5 minutes. Mix the cornstarch with the remaining Madeira, stir into the sauce with the remaining butter until thickened, then cook 3 minutes longer. Taste for seasoning.

Cut the fillet into ¾-inch slices, pour a little sauce over it, and serve the rest in a sauceboat.

Serves 8.

Serve with a red Bordeaux or Burgundy, or a red Rhône wine like Châteauneuf-du-Pape.

FILET MIGNON AUX CHAMPIGNONS
FILLET OF BEEF WITH MUSHROOMS

6 tablespoons butter	1 cup heavy cream
1 pound mushrooms, sliced	6 fillets of beef, ¾ inch thick
2 tablespoons flour	1/3 cup Madeira or
2 teaspoons salt	sweet sherry
½ teaspoon freshly ground black pepper	

Melt 3 tablespoons butter in a skillet; sauté the mushrooms 5 minutes. Stir in the flour, 1 teaspoon of the salt, and ¼ teaspoon pepper. Add the cream, stirring steadily to the boiling point. Reduce heat. Cook over low heat 5 minutes.

Melt the remaining butter in a skillet, and cook the fillets over high heat 3 minutes on each side. Season with remaining salt and pepper, add the wine, and bring to a boil.

To serve, arrange mushroom mixture in the center of a serving dish with the fillets around it.

Serves 6.

Serve with a Beaujolais, a dry red Bordeaux, or a dry Italian red wine like Valpolicella.

FILET DE BOEUF PÔELÉ
PAN-ROASTED FILLET OF BEEF

1 tablespoon olive oil	1 cup Brown Sauce
4-5-pound fillet of beef	(see recipe)
1 carrot, sliced	½ cup Madeira or
¾ cup sliced onion	sweet sherry

Heat the oil in a Dutch oven or heavy roasting pan; cook the meat in it over high heat until browned on all sides. Add the carrot and onion, and brown lightly. Add the Brown Sauce and wine. Cover. Roast in a 375° oven, allowing 12 minutes a pound for rare meat, 15 for medium, and 18 for well done. Baste occasionally. Put meat on a hot serving platter. Skim fat from pan juices, taste for seasoning, and serve in a sauceboat.

Serves 8-10.

Serve with a red Bordeaux or Burgundy, a red Rhône wine like Châteauneuf-du-Pape, or a dry Italian red wine like Grignolino.

LOMO DE TORO
MARINATED FILLETS OF BEEF

6 fillets of beef, cut	1 teaspoon salt
1 inch thick	½ teaspoon freshly ground
1/3 cup olive oil	black pepper
1 cup dry red wine	2 tablespoons flour
2 tablespoons wine vinegar	3 tablespoons butter
2 cloves garlic, minced	

Pound the beef lightly with a mallet or knife. Mix together the oil, vinegar, garlic, salt, and pepper; marinate the meat in it 4-6 hours, turning and basting frequently. Drain the meat, and dry on paper towels.

Mix the flour with a little of the marinade. Combine with all the marinade in a saucepan. Bring to a boil over low heat, stirring steadily, then cook 5 minutes longer.

Melt the butter in a skillet; cook the fillets in it over

high heat 2 minutes on each side, or to desired degree of rareness. Serve the sauce in a sauceboat.

Serves 6.

Serve with a dry red Bordeaux wine, a red Burgundy, including a Beaujolais, or a dry Italian red wine like Chianti.

MANZO BRASATO
BRAISED BEEF IN RED WINE

4 pounds eye round, or rump of beef	2 cloves garlic, minced
4 tablespoons olive oil	2 teaspoons salt
1 tablespoon butter	½ teaspoon freshly ground black pepper
2 cups dry red wine	½ teaspoon rosemary
1½ cups chopped onion	1 bay leaf
½ cup grated carrot	Dash ground cloves
½ cup diced celery	1½ cups diced tomatoes

Have the beef larded. Put all the ingredients in a Dutch oven or heavy saucepan. Cover tightly, bring to a boil, and cook over low heat 2½ hours or until tender. Discard bay leaf. Transfer the meat to a baking pan; purée the vegetables and gravy in a blender, or force through a sieve. Pour over the meat. Bake in a 450° over 15 minutes.

Serves 6-8.

Serve with a red Burgundy or Bordeaux, a red Rhône wine like Côte-Rôtie, or a red Italian wine like Chianti.

BEEF BOURGUIGNONNE
BEEF IN RED WINE

4 pounds rump or chuck of beef	1 cup grated carrot
½ cup flour	2 cloves garlic, minced
2½ teaspoons salt	3½ cups dry red wine
½ teaspoon freshly ground black pepper	2 tablespoons minced parsley
3 tablespoons olive oil	2 teaspoons finely chopped bay leaves
6 tablespoons butter	½ teaspoon marjoram
¼ cup warmed cognac	16 small white onions
2 slices salt pork, diced	1 teaspoon sugar
2 cups diced onions	16 mushroom caps

Cut the meat into 2-inch cubes; roll in a mixture of the flour, salt, and pepper. Heat the oil and 2 tablespoons butter in a skillet; brown the meat very well on all sides. Transfer to a casserole; pour the warmed cognac over it and set aflame.

Brown the salt pork in a skillet. Remove and add to the casserole. Pour off all but 2 tablespoons fat. In the remaining fat, sauté the diced onion slices, carrot, and garlic 5 minutes. Add to the meat, with the wine, parsley, bay leaves, and marjoram. Bring to a boil over direct heat, then cover and bake in a 350° oven 1 hour.

Melt the remaining butter in a skillet; add the onions and sugar. Brown lightly and remove. Sauté the mushrooms in the remaining butter 5 minutes. Add to the meat; re-cover, and bake 30 minutes longer, or until meat is tender. Taste for seasoning.

Serves 8-10.

Serve with a red Burgundy, including a Beaujolais, or a red Rhône wine like Châteauneuf-du-Pape.

STUFATO DI MANZO
BEEF WITH WHITE WINE

3 pounds eye round, cross rib, or rump	black pepper
	1½ cups dry white wine
4 tablespoons butter	1 cup peeled, diced tomatoes
3 cups thinly sliced onions	¾ cup sliced carrots
2 teaspoons salt	½ cup sliced celery
½ teaspoon freshly ground	½ teaspoon basil

Rinse the meat and pat dry. Melt the butter in a Dutch oven or heavy skillet; sauté the sliced onions until soft and yellow. Add the meat, and brown it on all sides. Season with the salt and pepper. Add the wine; cook over high heat 5 minutes. Add the tomatoes, carrots, celery, and basil. Bring to a boil, cover, and cook over low heat 2 hours, or until the meat is tender. Slice the meat and serve with the gravy.

Serves 6-8.

Serve with a red Bordeaux or Burgundy, a Rhône wine like Côte-Rôtie, or a dry Italian red wine like Barolo.

ESTOUFFAT CATALAN
BRAISED STEW, CATALAN STYLE

5-pound eye round of beef
2 cloves garlic, slivered
4 strips of salt pork
¼ cup vinegar
½ cup flour
1½ cups thinly sliced onion
2 carrots, cut in matchlike
     strips
2 small white turnips,
     peeled and quartered
3 tomatoes, peeled and diced

3 sprigs parsley ⎰ tied
1 bay leaf   ⎱ together
½ teaspoon thyme
2 cloves
2 teaspoons salt
½ teaspoon freshly ground
     black pepper
1 quart dry red wine
2 cups cooked or canned
     white beans

Cut a few slits in the beef and insert the garlic slivers,
then wrap with the salt pork. Brush the meat with the
vinegar and roll it in the flour. In a heavy deep casserole
or Dutch oven, spread the onion slices, carrots, turnips,
tomatoes, parsley and bay leaf, thyme, cloves, salt, and
pepper. Put the meat on top. Add the wine, bring to a boil
over direct heat, cover pan tightly, and bake in a 275°
oven 4 hours. When beef is almost cooked, add the beans
and bake 10 minutes longer. Discard bay leaf and parsley.
Serves 8-10.

Serve with a red Bordeaux or Burgundy, especially a
Beaujolais, or a Rhône wine like Châteauneuf-du-Pape, or
an Italian red wine like Chianti.

BOEUF EN MIROTON
PEASANT BEEF STEW

2 tablespoons butter
2 tablespoons flour
1 cup beef broth
1 cup dry red wine
1 teaspoon salt
½ teaspoon freshly ground
     black pepper
12 small white onions

6 potatoes, peeled and
     quartered
2 sprigs parsley
¼ teaspoon thyme
1 bay leaf
4 cups cooked beef, cut in
     ¼-inch cubes

Melt the butter in a saucepan; blend in the flour until
browned. Gradually mix in the broth and wine, stirring

steadily to the boiling point. Add the salt and pepper, onions, potatoes, parsley, thyme, and bay leaf. Cook over low heat 45 minutes. Add the beef. Cook 15 minutes longer. Discard parsley and bay leaf and serve.

Serves 6.

Serve with a red Bordeaux or Burgundy, a red Rhône wine like Côte-Rôtie, or a red Italian wine like Grignolino.

LA CARBONNADE
BEEF STEW, LANGUEDOC STYLE

2 tablespoons butter	2 cups cooked drained rice
3 pounds rump or sirloin steak, cut into ½-inch cubes	1 cup cooked or canned corn kernels
1 cup sliced onion	½ cup finely sliced green pepper
2 tomatoes peeled and sliced thin	¼ teaspoon saffron
2 teaspoons salt	1 teaspoon brown sugar
¼ teaspoon freshly ground pepper	1 cup dry white wine
	⅛ teaspoon cinnamon

Melt the butter in a casserole or Dutch oven; brown the meat in it. Add the sliced onion and the tomatoes, salt and pepper; cover, and cook over high heat 10 minutes, shaking pan frequently to prevent meat from sticking. Mix in the rice and corn, green pepper, saffron, sugar, wine, and cinnamon. Cover, and cook over low heat 15 minutes. Taste for seasoning.

Serves 6.

Serve with a red Bordeaux or a red Burgundy, including a Beaujolais, a red Rhône wine like Châteauneuf-du-Pape, or an Italian red wine like Barolo.

BOEUF À LA CATALANE
BEEF STEW WITH RICE

3 pounds rump or chuck of beef	1 cup dry white wine
¼ pound bacon	2 cups beef broth
3 tablespoons olive oil	2 teaspoons finely chopped bay leaves
2 teaspoons salt	½ teaspoon thyme
½ teaspoon freshly ground black pepper	2 cloves garlic, minced
1½ cups sliced onion	⅛ teaspoon saffron
1 cup raw rice	1½ cups peeled, chopped tomatoes

Cut the beef in 2-inch squares, 1 inch thick. Cook the bacon slices in boiling water 10 minutes, drain, dry, and cut in 1-inch pieces. Brown the bacon in a skillet; drain, and transfer to a casserole. Pour off the fat. Heat the oil in the skillet; brown the meat in it. Transfer to the casserole. Sprinkle with the salt and pepper. In the fat remaining in the skillet, sauté the onion slices 5 minutes. Transfer to the casserole. To the fat remaining, add the rice. Cook over medium heat, stirring constantly, until rice is translucent. Remove rice and reserve.

Add the wine to the skillet; bring to a boil, scraping the bottom of any browned particles. Add to the casserole with the broth, bay leaves, thyme, garlic, and saffron. Bring to a boil, cover, and bake in a 325° oven 1 hour. Mix in the tomatoes; re-cover, and bake 1½ hours longer.

Place over direct heat; lightly stir in the rice, and a little boiling water if necessary. (At this point there should be about 2½ cups liquid.) Re-cover, and cook over low heat 20 minutes, or until rice is tender. Taste for seasoning.

Serves 6-8.

Serve with a red Bordeaux, a red Burgundy, including a Beaujolais, or a Rhône wine like Côte-Rôtie.

L'ESTOUFFAT DE BOEUF
BEEF STEW, GASCONY STYLE

4-pound eye round of beef
2 cloves garlic, slivered
2½ teaspoons salt
½ teaspoon freshly ground
    black pepper
1 slice salt pork
⅛ teaspoon cinnamon
⅛ teaspoon nutmeg
3 cloves

Sprig parsley ⎫
Piece of celery ⎬ tied
Bay leaf ⎭ together
(bouquet garni)
1 onion, quartered
2 carrots, cut in long strips
1 slice bacon, diced
2 shallots
¼ cup cognac
½ cup beef broth
2 cups dry red wine

Cut slits in the meat and insert the garlic slivers; rub
the meat with the salt and pepper. Put the salt pork in a
large casserole or Dutch oven and place the beef over it.
Add the cinnamon, nutmeg, cloves, bouquet garni, onion,
carrots, diced bacon, shallots, cognac, broth, and wine. The
liquid should almost cover the meat. Cover casserole with
a piece of aluminum foil and tie securely. Cover with lid,
and roast in a 350° oven 1 hour. Reduce heat to 250° and
roast 5 hours longer. Skim fat from gravy before serving.
If you like, prepare the meat the day before it is to be
served and reheat—the flavor will be even better.

Serves 6-8.

Serve with a dry red Bordeaux or Burgundy, or a dry
Italian red wine like Bardolino, or a red Rhône wine like
Châteauneuf-du-Pape.

BOEUF EN DAUBE

4 pounds chuck or rump
    of beef
3 tablespoons flour
1 teaspoon salt
½ teaspoon freshly ground
    black pepper
⅛ teaspoon nutmeg

¼ pound salt pork, diced
½ cup chopped onion
½ cup grated carrot
2 cups dry red wine
1 cup beef broth
½ teaspoon thyme
1 bay leaf

Cut the beef in 1½-inch cubes. Toss in a mixture of the
flour, salt, pepper, and nutmeg.

Brown the salt pork in a Dutch oven or casserole; drain off all but 3 tablespoons fat. Add the onion, carrot, and beef; cook over medium heat until well browned. Add the wine, broth, thyme, and bay leaf. Cover, and cook over low heat 1½ hours, or until the meat is tender. Skim off the fat; taste for seasoning.

Serves 8-10.

Serve with a heavy red Bordeaux, Beaujolais or other red Burgundy, a red Rhône like Châteauneuf-du-Pape, or a dry red Italian wine like Barolo.

RAGOÛT DE BOEUF BORDELAISE
MARINATED BEEF STEW

1 clove garlic, minced	½ cup flour
2 teaspoons salt	¼ cup olive oil
½ teaspoon freshly ground black pepper	2 cups beef broth
	3 sprigs parsley
2 cloves	12 small white onions
1 bay leaf	1½ cups sliced carrots
¼ teaspoon thyme	12 mushroom caps
1 cup dry red wine	1 cup cooked green beans
3 pounds chuck or rump of beef, cut in 2-inch cubes	

In a glass or pottery bowl, combine the garlic, salt, pepper, cloves, bay leaf, thyme, and wine. Add the meat and marinate 4 hours, or overnight if possible. Drain the meat, reserving the marinade. Toss the meat with the flour.

Heat the oil in a deep casserole or Dutch oven; add meat, and cook over low heat until very dark brown. Mix in the reserved marinade, broth, and parsley; bring to a boil, and cook over high heat 15 minutes. Reduce heat, cover, and cook over low heat 30 minutes. Add the onions, carrots, and mushrooms. Re-cover, and cook over low heat 1½ hours, or until meat is tender. Mix in beans, taste for seasoning, and cook 2 minutes.

Serves 6-8.

Serve with a red Bordeaux, a dry red Burgundy wine, including a Beaujolais, or a red Italian wine like Valpolicella.

CARBONADA CRIOLLA
MEAT AND FRUIT STEW, SOUTH AMERICAN STYLE

4 tablespoons olive oil
2 tablespoons butter
2 pounds beef, cut in 1-inch cubes
1 pound veal, cut in 1-inch cubes
1½ cups diced onion
1½ cups dry white wine
1 tablespoon tomato paste
1 bay leaf
2 teaspoons salt
½ teaspoon freshly ground black pepper
½ teaspoon thyme
1 cup beef broth
2 cups cubed sweet potatoes
2 pears, cubed
2 peaches or apples, peeled and sliced
3 tablespoons seedless raisins
½ cup diced bananas

Heat the oil and butter in a heavy casserole; brown the beef and veal in it. Remove meat. Brown the onion in the fat remaining in the pan. Return the meat, and stir in the wine, tomato paste, bay leaf, salt, pepper, thyme, and broth. Bring to a boil, cover, and cook over low heat 1 hour. Add the sweet potatoes; re-cover, and cook 30 minutes. Carefully mix in the pears, peaches or apples, and raisins. Cook 10 minutes. Taste for seasoning, sprinkle with the bananas, and serve with rice.

Serves 8-10.

Serve with a red Bordeaux or Burgundy, or an Italian red wine.

BOEUF À LA MODE

5 pounds rump, sirloin tip, or eye round
2½ teaspoons salt
¼ teaspoon freshly ground black pepper
1 cup thinly sliced onion
1 cup sliced carrot
2 cloves garlic, sliced
2 teaspoons thyme
¼ cup minced parsley
2 bay leaves
4 cups dry red wine
¼ cup cognac
¼ cup olive oil
2 tablespoons vegetable oil
2 cups beef broth
1 veal knuckle, cracked
1 teaspoon Worcestershire sauce
1 tablespoon cornstarch
2 tablespoons sweet sherry

Have the beef larded; rub with the salt and pepper. In a large glass or pottery bowl, spread half the onion, carrot, garlic, thyme, parsley, and bay leaves. Put the meat in the bowl and cover with the remaining vegetables and herbs. Mix together the red wine, cognac, and olive oil; pour over the meat. Cover, and marinate in the refrigerator 24 hours, or 5 hours at room temperature. Turn and baste meat frequently. Drain the meat thoroughly, then dry with paper towels. Heat the marinade.

Heat the vegetable oil in a Dutch oven or heavy casserole; brown the meat on all sides. Pour off the fat. Add the heated marinade. Cook over high heat until marinade is reduced to half. Add the broth and veal knuckle. Bring to a boil, skim the top, cover, and bake in a 325° oven 3½ hours, turning the meat several times. Transfer the meat to a heated serving dish and keep warm; discard veal knuckle and bay leaves. Mix the Worcestershire sauce, cornstarch, and sherry until smooth; stir into the gravy until thickened. Serve in a sauceboat. Sautéed small white onions and braised carrot quarters may be arranged around the meat, if desired.

Serves 10-12.

Serve with a red Burgundy, especially Beaujolais, a red Rhône wine like Châteauneuf-du-Pape, or an Italian red wine like Bardolino.

STUFATINO ALLA ROMANA
BEEF STEW, ROMAN STYLE

3 pounds eye round of beef	2 tablespoons butter
3 tablespoons flour	1 cup thinly sliced onion
2 teaspoons salt	2 cloves garlic, minced
½ teaspoon freshly ground black pepper	1 cup dry red wine
	1 tablespoon tomato paste
½ teaspoon rosemary	½ cup boiling water
2 slices salt pork, diced	

Cut the meat in 1-inch slices. Sprinkle with the flour, salt, pepper, and rosemary. Lightly brown the salt pork in a heavy casserole. Pour off all but 2 tablespoons of the fat. Add the butter, onion slices, and garlic; sauté 5 minutes. Add the meat; cook over medium heat until browned on

both sides. Stir in the wine; cook over high heat 5 minutes.
Blend in the tomato paste, mixed with the water. Cover,
and cook over low heat 1½ hours. Taste for seasoning.
Serves 6-8.

Serve with any Italian red wine, especially Chianti or
Bardolino, a red Bordeaux or Burgundy, or a red Rhône
wine like Châteauneuf-du-Pape.

LE HACHUA
BRAISED BEEF

¼ cup olive oil	1 bay leaf
3 pounds rump or chuck of beef, cut in 1-inch cubes	½ teaspoon thyme
	2 teaspoons salt
2 tablespoons flour	½ teaspoon freshly ground pepper
2 cups chopped onion	
2 cloves garlic, minced	1 cup hot water
1½ cups finely diced ham	1½ cups dry white wine
3 sprigs parsley	3 green peppers, cut julienne

Heat the oil in a casserole or Dutch oven; brown the
beef in it on all sides. Blend in the flour; add onion, garlic
ham, parsley, bay leaf, thyme, salt, and pepper. Cook 5
minutes, stirring frequently. Gradually stir in the water
and wine. Cover tightly, and bake in a 275° oven 2 hours.
Add the green peppers; re-cover and bake 30 minutes
longer, or until the meat is tender.
Serves 6-8.

Serve with a red Bordeaux or Burgundy, especially a
Beaujolais, a Rhône red wine like Hermitage, or a dry
Italian red wine like Chianti.

GRYTSTEK
SWEDISH POT ROAST

4 pounds eye round or rump of beef	¼ cup cognac
2½ teaspoons salt	1 cup boiling water
¾ teaspoon freshly ground black pepper	1 cup dry white wine
	¼ teaspoon allspice
4 tablespoons butter	2 bay leaves
1½ cups chopped onion	2 teaspoons anchovy paste
2 carrots, sliced	1 tablespoon cider vinegar
¼ cup molasses	2 tablespoons flour
	1½ cups light cream

Rub the meat with salt and pepper. Melt the butter in a Dutch oven or heavy saucepan; brown the meat well on all sides. Add the onion and carrot, and cook 10 minutes. Stir in the molasses, cognac, water, wine, allspice, bay leaves, anchovy paste, and vinegar. Cover, and cook over low heat 2½ hours, or until tender. Transfer the meat to a heated platter. Mix the flour and cream until smooth; blend into the gravy, stirring steadily to the boiling point. Cook 5 minutes. Discard bay leaves, taste for seasoning, and serve gravy separately.

Serves 8-10.

Serve with a red Burgundy, Bordeaux, a Rhône wine like Côte-Rôtie, or an Italian red wine.

MANZO IN SALSA DI PREZZEMOLA
BEEF WITH PARSLEY SAUCE

4 slices eye round of beef, cut 2 inches thick	¼ cup chopped parsley
	¾ cup dry white wine
2 tablespoons olive oil	½ teaspoon salt
4 anchovy fillets, chopped	¼ teaspoon freshly ground black pepper
1 clove garlic, minced	

Pound the beef with a mallet or cleaver to tenderize. Heat the oil in a skillet; brown the beef on both sides. Mix in the anchovies, garlic, and parsley; cook over low heat 5 minutes. Add the wine, salt, and pepper. Cover, and cook over low heat 30 minutes or until meat is tender.

Serves 4.

Serve with any dry red Bordeaux or Burgundy.

TOURNEDOS LYONNAISE
BEEF TENDERLOIN, LYONS STYLE

4 fillets of beef, cut 1 inch thick	4 slices sautéed French bread
1½ teaspoons salt	2 tablespoons chopped shallots or onion
½ teaspoon freshly ground black pepper	½ cup dry white wine
4 tablespoons butter	1 teaspoon anchovy paste

Rub the fillets with salt and pepper. Melt 3 tablespoons of the butter in a skillet; cook the fillets in it over high heat 2 minutes on each side, or to desired degree of rareness. Place a fillet on a sautéed slice of bread. Keep hot. Add the shallots to butter remaining in the pan; sauté 1 minute. Stir in the wine, anchovy paste, and the remaining tablespoon butter. Cook 2 minutes, stirring frequently. Pour sauce over the fillets, and serve with sautéed potatoes. Serves 4.

Serve with a red Burgundy or Bordeaux, a dry red Italian wine like Bardolino, or a red Rhône wine like Hermitage.

CADERA DE TORO
BRAISED BEEF

4 pounds eye round of beef	2 cups dry white wine
2½ teaspoons salt	1 cup water
¾ teaspoon freshly ground black pepper	2 teaspoons wine vinegar
2 cloves garlic, minced	2 cloves
¼ cup olive oil	1 bay leaf
1 cup chopped onion	1 tablespoon unsweetened cocoa

Rub the meat with a mixture of the salt, pepper, and garlic. Heat the oil in a Dutch oven or heavy saucepan; brown the meat in it lightly. Add the chopped onions; cook 5 minutes, stirring frequently. Pour off the fat; add the wine, water, vinegar, cloves, and bay leaf. Cover, and cook over low heat 2½ hours, or until the meat is tender. Turn meat a few times, and add a little boiling water if necessary. Transfer the meat to a hot platter. Strain the gravy into a saucepan; stir the cocoa into it. Cook 1 minute. Slice the meat, and pour the gravy over it.

Serves 6-8.

Serve with a red Bordeaux or Burgundy, a dry Italian red wine like Valpolicella, or a red Rhône wine like Hermitage.

SWISS STEAK IN WINE SAUCE

¼ cup flour	1 cup chopped onion
1½ teaspoons salt	1 clove garlic, minced
¼ teaspoon freshly ground black pepper	1 cup dry red wine
	½ teaspoon marjoram
4 pounds round steak	1 bay leaf
4 tablespoons butter	

Mix together the flour, salt, and pepper. Dip the steak in the mixture, then pound the mixture in. Melt the butter in a Dutch oven or heavy saucepan. Brown the steak in it on both sides. Add the onion and garlic. Continue browning for 5 minutes. Add the wine, marjoram, and bay leaf. Cover and cook over low heat for 2 hours, basting and turning the meat frequently. Taste for seasoning. Discard the bay leaf.

Serves 6.

Serve with a red Bordeaux or Burgundy, or any dry Italian red wine like Bardolino.

BEEF BIRDS

1½ pounds fillet of beef	¼ cup grated Swiss cheese
1¼ teaspoons salt	3 tablespoons butter
½ teaspoon freshly ground black pepper	1 clove garlic, minced
	1½ cups peeled, chopped tomatoes
½ teaspoon thyme	
⅛ teaspoon nutmeg	¼ pound mushrooms, sliced
¼ pound ham, chopped	1 bay leaf
¼ cup chopped parsley	¾ cup dry white wine

Slice the beef as thin as possible, then pound between two sheets of waxed paper. Season one side with the salt, pepper, thyme, and nutmeg. On the unseasoned side, spread a mixture of the ham, parsley, and cheese. Roll up, and fasten with toothpicks or tie with white thread.

Melt the butter in a casserole or deep skillet; brown the meat rolls on all sides. Mix in the garlic, tomatoes, mushrooms, bay leaf, and wine. Bring to a boil, and cook over low heat 20 minutes. Taste for seasoning. Discard bay leaf.

Serves 6-8.

Serve with any red Bordeaux or Burgundy.

BEEF STROGANOFF

2½ pounds fillet of beef	½ cup Madeira or sweet sherry
4 tablespoons butter	
2 tablespoons vegetable oil	¼ cup beef broth
½ pound mushrooms, sliced	1¾ teaspoons salt
3 tablespoons minced shallots or green onions	½ teaspoon freshly ground black pepper
	1 cup sour cream

Trim the fat off the fillet. Slice ½ inch thick, then cut into pieces 2 inches long and 2 inches wide.

Heat 2 tablespoons butter and 1 tablespoon oil in a skillet; sauté the mushrooms over medium heat 3 minutes. Add the shallots; sauté 2 minutes. Remove from the skillet. Add the remaining butter and oil to the skillet. Bring to a boil, then add the meat. Brown quickly over high heat. Remove the meat, and pour off the fat.

Mix the wine and broth into the skillet, scraping the bottom well; cook over high heat 2 minutes. Season the meat with the salt and pepper, then return to the skillet with the mushrooms. Cook over low heat 5 minutes, stirring frequently. Just before serving, blend in sour cream. Heat, but do not let boil.

Serves 4-6.

Serve with a red Bordeaux or Burgundy.

NOODLES WITH STROGANOFF SAUCE

4 tablespoons butter
¼ cup chopped green onions
1 clove garlic, minced
½ pound mushrooms, sliced
1 pound ground beef
2 tablespoons lemon juice
1 cup dry red wine
¼ cup beef broth

1 teaspoon salt
¼ teaspoon freshly ground
   black pepper
½ pound medium noodles,
   half cooked and drained
1 cup sour cream
3 tablespoons chopped
   parsley

Melt the butter in a large skillet; sauté the green onions, garlic, and mushrooms 5 minutes. Add the beef; cook over medium heat, stirring almost constantly, until meat browns. Mix in the lemon juice, wine, broth, salt, and pepper. Bring to a boil, and cook over low heat 15 minutes. Add the half-cooked noodles; cover, and cook 5 minutes. Blend in the sour cream, taste for seasoning, and reheat, but do not let boil. Sprinkle with the parsley.

Serves 4.

Serve with a *rosé* wine, or any light dry red wine.

BEEF AND PRUNES WITH SPAGHETTI

½ cup olive oil
1 cup chopped onion
2 cloves garlic, minced
1 pound beef, cut in ½-inch
   cubes
2 8-ounce cans tomato sauce
¾ cup dry red wine

½ teaspoon salt
½ teaspoon nutmeg
12 prunes, pre-soaked and
   pitted
1 pound spaghetti, cooked
   and drained
½ cup grated Parmesan cheese

Heat the oil in a saucepan; sauté the onion, garlic, and beef until browned, stirring frequently. Add the tomato sauce, wine, salt, and nutmeg. Cook over low heat 40 minutes. Add the prunes. Cook 30 minutes. Taste for seasoning.

Heap the cooked spaghetti on a platter and pour the meat mixture over it. Serve with the cheese.

Serves 4-6.

Serve with any dry red Bordeaux or Burgundy.

BEEF AND MACARONI CASSEROLE

¼ cup olive oil
1½ cups chopped onion
1 clove garlic, minced
1½ pounds ground beef
1 cup peeled chopped
    tomatoes
¾ cup dry red wine
2½ teaspoons salt
¼ teaspoon freshly ground
    black pepper

½ teaspoon basil
1 cup sliced almonds
3 eggs
½ cup grated Parmesan cheese
1 pound elbow macaroni,
    cooked and drained
2 egg yolks
½ cup cream

Heat the olive oil in a skillet; sauté the onion and garlic 10 minutes. Add beef and sauté 10 minutes, stirring almost constantly. Mix in the tomatoes, wine, 1½ teaspoons salt, the pepper, and basil. Cook over medium heat 15 minutes. Stir in the almonds.

Beat the eggs; stir in the cheese and spaghetti. Spread half the spaghetti mixture in a 2-quart buttered casserole. Spread the meat mixture over it. Cover with the remaining spaghetti mixture. Beat together the egg yolks, cream, and remaining salt, and pour over top. Bake in a 350° oven 25 minutes, or until custard is set and lightly browned. Serves 6-8.

Serve with a dry red Italian wine like Barolo, or a red Bordeaux or Burgundy.

STEAK DIANE

2 8-ounce club steaks, cut
    ¼ inch thick
1 teaspoon dry mustard
2 tablespoons A.1. Sauce
4 tablespoons butter

2 tablespoons warm cognac
⅓ cup dry sherry
1 tablespoon chopped chives
    or green onions

Trim the steaks, then rub with a mixture of the mustard and A.1. Sauce. Melt 2 tablespoons butter in a skillet or chafing dish. Add the steaks and cook over high heat 2 minutes on each side, or to desired degree of rareness. Set the cognac aflame in a ladle and pour over the steaks. Immediately add the sherry, chives, and remaining butter.

Transfer the steaks to a hot serving dish, bring the sauce to a boil, and pour over the steaks.

Serves 2.

Serve with a red Burgundy or Bordeaux, a red Rhône wine like Hermitage, or an Italian red wine like Chianti.

SLICED BEEF WITH CHICKEN LIVER SAUCE

2 pounds fillet of beef	¼ teaspoon freshly ground
4 tablespoons butter	black pepper
½ pound chicken livers	⅓ cup dry sherry
1 bay leaf	¼ cup beef broth
1 teaspoon salt	2 tablespoons cognac

Cut the meat in thin strips across the grain.

Melt 2 tablespoons butter in a skillet; sauté the livers and bay leaf over high heat 3 minutes. Sprinkle with the salt and pepper; sauté 2 minutes. Discard the bay leaf; purée the livers, sherry, and broth in an electric blender until smooth, or force through a food mill. Return purée to skillet, and keep it warm while preparing the meat.

Melt the remaining butter in a skillet; sauté the meat over high heat 2 minutes, shaking the pan frequently. Heat the cognac and pour over the meat; set aflame. Transfer the meat to a heated serving dish and pour the liver sauce over it.

Serves 4-6.

Serve with a red Burgundy or Bordeaux, a red Rhône wine like Châteauneuf-du-Pape, or a dry Italian red wine like Grignolino or Barolo.

STEAK AND KIDNEY PIE

4 veal kidneys	¾ teaspoon freshly ground
2 pounds top round steak	black pepper
¼ cup flour	½ teaspoon thyme
3 tablespoons vegetable oil	1 tablespoon tomato paste
1 cup thinly sliced onion	1 cup dry red wine
½ pound mushrooms, sliced	Pastry for 1-crust pie
2 teaspoons salt	

Wash the kidneys, cut in half, and discard the core. Cover with boiling water, let stand 2 minutes, drain, and cube.

Cut the steak into 1½-inch cubes. Toss the meat and kidneys with the flour. Heat the oil in a skillet; brown the meat and kidneys in it.

In a buttered 2-quart casserole, arrange layers of the sautéed meats, the sliced onion, and the mushrooms. Mix together the salt, pepper, thyme, tomato paste, and wine; pour into the casserole. Cover the casserole and bake in a 350° oven 2½ hours.

Prepare the pastry and roll out a little larger than the casserole. Taste casserole contents for seasoning. Carefully place the pastry over the meat mixture and press the edges down with a fork. Make a few gashes in the top. Increase the heat to 400° and bake 25 minutes longer, or until the pastry is browned.

Serves 4-6.

Serve with a red Bordeaux or Burgundy, or an Italian red wine like Valpolicella.

MEAT BALL CASSEROLE

4 tablespoons butter	½ teaspoon freshly ground
1 cup chopped onion	black pepper
1 clove garlic, minced	½ teaspoon thyme
½ cup dry bread crumbs	2 tablespoons vegetable oil
2 pounds ground beef	1 pound mushrooms, sliced
2 eggs, beaten	1 10½-ounce can cream of
2 teaspoons salt	mushroom soup
	2 cups dry white wine

Melt 2 tablespoons butter in a skillet; sauté the onion 10 minutes. Mix in the garlic and bread crumbs; sauté 2 minutes. Remove from heat, and add the beef, eggs, salt, pepper, and thyme. Mix well. Shape into 2-inch balls.

Heat the oil and remaining butter in a skillet; brown the meat balls in it. Transfer to a casserole or baking dish. Sautée the mushrooms in the fat remaining in the skillet for 3 minutes. Add to the casserole. Mix the soup and wine; pour over the meat balls. Cover casserole; bake in

a 350° oven 45 minutes, removing the cover for the last
10 minutes. Taste for seasoning.

Serves 6-8.

Serve with a red Bordeaux or a red Burgundy, including
a Beaujolais, an Italian red wine like Chianti, or a red
Rhône wine like Hermitage.

LUK AWALIANI
MEAT-STUFFED ONIONS, SYRIAN STYLE

12 large onions
¾ pound ground beef
¾ pound ground lamb
½ pound calf's or beef liver,
    ground
¾ cup chopped mixed nuts
1½ teaspoons salt
½ teaspoon freshly ground
    black pepper

⅛ teaspoon nutmeg
4 cups beef broth
2½ cups strained canned
    plum tomatoes
1 cup chopped mushrooms
1 cup sour cream
½ cup sherry

Peel the onions and carefully remove as much of the
centers as possible. Reserve. Mix together the beef, lamb,
liver, nuts, salt, pepper, and nutmeg. Stuff the onions with
the mixture, piled high. Arrange in a baking pan. Pour the
broth and 2 cups tomatoes around them. Bake in a 350°
oven 1 hour. While they are baking, prepare the sauce.

Chop the onion centers, and combine in a saucepan
with the mushrooms, sour cream, sherry, and remaining
tomatoes. Cover, and cook over low heat 20 minutes. Add
the onions. Bake 30 minutes longer, basting frequently.
Taste for seasoning.

Serves 6-12.

CHIPPED BEEF WITH ARTICHOKE HEARTS

6 tablespoons butter
6 tablespoons flour
1½ cups milk, scalded
Salt, depending on the saltiness
    of the chipped beef
2 cups sour cream

½ cup dry white wine
2 cups shredded chipped beef
1 package frozen artichoke
    hearts, cooked and
    drained
1½ cups sliced ripe olives

Melt the butter in a saucepan; blend in the flour until smooth. Add the milk, stirring vigorously with a wire whisk. Cook until thick and smooth, then add the salt, sour cream, wine, beef, artichokes, and olives.

Heat, but do not boil. Serve hot with cooked rice.

Serves 4.

Serve with any dry red Bordeaux or Burgundy.

THREE-MEAT GOULASH

4 tablespoons butter	2 teaspoons salt
3 cups thinly sliced onions	½ teaspoon freshly ground
1 pound boneless beef, cut in	black pepper
1-inch cubes	2 teaspoons paprika
1 pound boneless veal, cut in	2 tablespoons tomato paste
1-inch cubes	1 cup dry white wine
1 pound boneless pork, cut in	1 cup sour cream
1-inch cubes	

Melt the butter in a casserole; sauté the sliced onions 10 minutes. Add all the meat, and cook over medium heat until browned. Stir in the salt, pepper, paprika, tomato paste, and ¼ cup wine. Cover, and cook over low heat 30 minutes. Add the remaining wine, and cook 1½ hours longer. Stir the sour cream into the pan juices. Heat, but do not let boil.

Serves 6-8.

Serve with a red Bordeaux or Burgundy, an Italian red wine like Valpolicello, or if you wish, with a *rosé*.

ROAST LEG OF LAMB

4-pound leg of lamb	¾ teaspoon freshly ground
3 cloves garlic, cut in slivers	black pepper
¾ teaspoon rosemary	4 tablespoons butter
2½ teaspoons salt	1½ cups dry vermouth

Make a few slits in the lamb and insert the garlic and rosemary. Rub the leg with the salt and pepper. Place in a shallow roasting pan and dot with the butter. Roast in a 450° oven 25 minutes, or until browned. Pour off the fat.

Add the vermouth. Reduce heat to 350°, and roast 1 hour longer, or until meat is tender; baste frequently.

Serves 4-6.

Serve with any red Bordeaux or Burgundy.

MARINATED ROAST LAMB

4-5-pound leg of lamb	1 teaspoon rosemary
1 tablespoon salt	½ cup olive oil
¾ teaspoon freshly ground	⅓ cup wine vinegar
black pepper	1 cup dry red wine

Trim the fat off the lamb. Prick the lamb in several places, then rub with the salt, pepper, and rosemary. Place in a large glass bowl, and pour over it a mixture of the oil, vinegar, and wine. Marinate in the refrigerator 8 hours, basting occasionally.

Drain, and place in a shallow roasting pan. Roast in a 350° oven, allowing 15 minutes a pound, or to desired degree of rareness. Add the marinade after 30 minutes roasting time, and baste frequently thereafter.

Serves 6-8.

Serve with any red Bordeaux or Burgundy, or any dry Italian red wine.

ROAST CROWN OF LAMB

Crown of lamb	2 cups fresh bread crumbs
½ teaspoon thyme	½ cup melted butter
3 teaspoons salt	2 cloves garlic, minced
¾ teaspoon freshly ground	1½ cups dry sherry
black pepper	Sautéed mushroom caps
½ cup minced onion	

Have the butcher shape a crown for you — it will require 16 ribs, so plan to serve it for at least 8 people. Have the bones scraped, and the meat from them ground. Mix the ground meat with the thyme, ¾ teaspoon salt, ¼ teaspoon pepper, the minced onion, bread crumbs, and ¼ cup of the melted butter.

Rub the crown with a mixture of the garlic and remaining salt and pepper. Place in a roasting pan and fill the center with the stuffing. Cover the stuffing with a piece of aluminum foil. Place a potato cube or a piece of salt pork on each bone to keep ends from burning. Roast in a 450° oven 20 minutes. Pour off the fat, and add the remaining butter and sherry. Reduce heat to 350°, and roast 2 hours longer, or to desired degree of rareness. Baste frequently, and remove foil from stuffing for last 15 minutes of roasting time. Transfer to a heated platter, remove potato or pork and replace each piece with a mushroom cap. Skim the fat from the gravy, and serve gravy with the roast.

Serves 8-10.

Serve with any red Bordeaux or Burgundy.

ROAST SADDLE OF LAMB

7-pound loin of lamb, in one piece	¾ teaspoon freshly ground black pepper
2½ teaspoons salt	2 cloves garlic, minced
	1 cup dry red wine

Have the flank ends rolled and tied by the butcher. Rub the lamb with a mixture of the salt, pepper, and garlic. Place in a shallow roasting pan. Roast in a 400° oven 20 minutes. Pour off the fat. Add the wine; roast 1½ hours longer, or to desired degree of rareness, basting frequently. Carve parallel to the bones in long strips — don't cut into chops.

Serves 6-8.

Serve with a red Bordeaux or Burgundy, or any dry Italian red wine like Barolo.

KZARTMA
SHANKS OF LAMB, NEAR EAST STYLE

6 lamb shanks	⅛ teaspoon oregano
1 cup chopped onion	2 tablespoons paprika
2 tablespoons butter	3 cloves garlic, minced
1 tablespoon salt	1 8-ounce can tomato sauce
1 teaspoon freshly ground black pepper	½ cup beef broth
	½ cup dry sherry

Soak the shanks in cold water for ½ hour. Drain, dry, and remove excess fat. Arrange in a shallow casserole or deep skillet with ovenproof handle.

Sauté the chopped onion in the butter and add to the lamb with the salt, pepper, oregano, paprika, garlic, tomato sauce, broth, and sherry. Cover, and bake in a 350° oven 1½ hours, basting occasionally. Remove cover and continue baking in a 250° oven until lamb browns and is tender — about 45 minutes. Baste frequently. Serve with cracked wheat or rice.

Serves 6-8.

SHISH KABOB

¼ cup dry red wine	1 tablespoon salt
¼ cup olive oil	2 pounds boneless lamb, cut
2 tablespoons grated onion	in 1½-inch cubes
1 teaspoon crushed coriander	Sliced onions
seeds	Sliced tomatoes
1 teaspoon ground ginger	Sliced green peppers
1 teaspoon turmeric	Mushroom caps
1 clove garlic, minced	½ cup melted butter

Mix together the wine, oil, grated onion, crushed coriander seeds, ginger, tumeric, garlic, and salt. Marinate the meat in the mixture for 2 hours. Use 6 skewers and alternately thread the meat, sliced onions, tomatoes, green peppers, and mushroom caps on them, starting and ending with meat. Broil over charcoal or in the oven broiler, turning the skewers frequently and basting with the butter. Broil 10 minutes, or to desired degree of rareness.

Serves 6.

Note: Beef or pork are equally good prepared in this way.

ARMENIAN SHISH KABOB

1½ pounds boneless leg of
    lamb
1½ cups dry red wine
1⅓ cups sherry
¼ teaspoon thyme
½ teaspoon marjoram
½ teaspoon Tabasco
½ teaspoon salt

2 onions, thinly sliced
18 small white onions
18 mushroom caps
18 squares green pepper
18 cubes eggplant
½ cup canned mushroom
    sauce

Cut the lamb in 1-inch cubes. In a glass or pottery bowl, combine the red wine, 1 cup sherry, thyme, marjoram, Tabasco, salt, and sliced onions. Add the meat. Marinate in the refrigerator 24 hours. Drain.

On 6 skewers, alternately thread the meat, white onions, mushrooms, green pepper, and eggplant. Mix the remaining sherry with the mushroom sauce, and brush the skewered ingredients.

Broil 15 minutes, turning the skewers frequently. Serve with rice.

Serves 6.

LAMB IN SOUR-CREAM SAUCE

3 pounds boneless lamb, cut
    in 1-inch cubes
¼ cup flour
2 teaspoons salt
½ teaspoon freshly ground
    black pepper
⅛ teaspoon rosemary

3 tablespoons butter
1 cup chopped onion
3 tablespoons dry sherry
1 cup dry white wine
½ cup beef broth
1 cup sour cream

Roll the lamb in a mixture of the flour, salt, pepper, and rosemary. Melt the butter in a Dutch oven or heavy skillet; brown the lamb in it. Pour off the fat. Mix in the chopped onions; cook over low heat 3 minutes. Add the sherry; cook until evaporated. Add the white wine and broth; cover, and cook over low heat 1½ hours, or until the lamb is tender. Mix in the sour cream; taste for seasoning. Heat, but do not let boil.

Serves 6-8.

Serve with a dry Italian red wine, or if you wish, with a *rosé*.

ABBACCHIO AL VERMOUTH
LAMB WITH ARTICHOKES IN VERMOUTH

2 tablespoons butter
3 pounds shoulder of lamb, cut in 1-inch cubes
2½ teaspoons salt
¼ teaspoon freshly ground black pepper
¼ cup dry vermouth

1 package frozen artichoke hearts, cooked and drained
4 eggs
½ cup grated Parmesan cheese
2 tablespoons minced parsley

Melt the butter in a casserole or deep skillet with oven-proof handle. Brown the lamb in it. Season with 2 tea-spoons salt and the pepper. Add the wine; cook over high heat 5 minutes. Cover, and bake in a 350° oven 35 min-utes; add the artichokes, and a little boiling water if neces-sary. Re-cover, and bake 10 minutes.

Beat together the eggs, cheese, parsley, and remaining salt. Pour over the lamb and artichokes. Bake, uncovered, 10 minutes longer.

Serves 6.

Serve with a red Bordeaux or Burgundy, or a *rosé*.

AGNEAU À LA RHEIMS
ROAST LAMB IN CHAMPAGNE SAUCE

6-pound leg of lamb
1 tablespoon salt
1 teaspoon freshly ground black pepper
¼ cup flour

4 tablespoons butter
½ cup beef broth
1½ cups champagne
½ cup grated onion
1 clove garlic, minced

Remove the fell (skin) of the lamb, and trim the fat. Rub the leg with a mixture of the salt, pepper, and flour. Place in a roasting pan, and dot with the butter. Roast in a 450° oven for 20 minutes. Combine the broth, champagne, grated onion, and garlic in a saucepan. Bring to a boil, and pour over the lamb. Reduce the heat to 350°, and con-tinue roasting for 2½ hours, or until the lamb is tender, basting frequently. Skim the fat from the gravy, and serve gravy in a sauceboat.

Serves 6-8.

Serve with champagne or a *rosé*.

AGNEAU AU VIN ROUGE
LAMB STEW IN RED WINE

3 pounds boneless lamb, cut in 1½-inch cubes	3 tablespoons butter
¼ cup flour	3 tablespoons warmed cognac
2 teaspoons salt	3 cups dry red wine
¼ teaspoon freshly ground black pepper	2 cups diced onions
½ teaspoon thyme	1 cup diced carrots
	1 bay leaf

Roll the lamb in a mixture of the flour, salt, pepper, and thyme. Melt the butter in a casserole; brown the meat in it. Pour the warmed cognac over the meat and set it aflame. When flames die, add the wine, diced onion, carrots, and bay leaf. Cover, and bake in a 350° oven 2 hours. Skim off the fat and discard the bay leaf. If gravy is too thin, add 1 tablespoon flour, kneaded with 1 tablespoon butter. Cook over direct heat until thickened.

Serves 6-8.

Serve with any red Bordeaux or Burgundy, or a *rosé*.

DAUBE À LA MODE D'AVIGNON
LAMB IN RED WINE

3 pounds boneless lamb	½ teaspoon thyme
3 cups dry red wine	3 slices salt pork, diced
2 cloves garlic, minced	2 teaspoons salt
1½ cups diced onions	½ teaspoon freshly ground black pepper
3 teaspoons finely chopped bay leaves	1 cup peeled, diced tomatoes
3 peppercorns	3 tablespoons minced parsley

Cut the lamb in 1½-inch cubes. Combine the wine, garlic, diced onions, bay leaves, peppercorns, and thyme in a glass or pottery bowl. Marinate the lamb in the mixture 8 hours, basting occasionally.

Brown the salt pork in a casserole or Dutch oven; pour off the fat. Drain the lamb, reserving the marinade, and season with the salt and pepper. Add to salt pork, and cook over medium heat 10 minutes. Mix in 2 cups of the reserved marinade, the tomatoes, and parsley; cover tightly, and bake in a 300° oven 3 hours, adding a little of the remaining marinade from time to time if necessary. Skim the fat off the gravy. Taste for seasoning.

Serves 6-8.

Serve with a dry red Italian wine, or a red Bordeaux or Burgundy.

COSTOLETTE D'AGNELLO
LAMB CHOPS IN WHITE WINE

4 shoulder lamb chops, cut 1 inch thick	1 cup dry white wine
1½ teaspoons salt	½ teaspoon rosemary
½ teaspoon freshly ground black pepper	1 clove garlic, minced
2 tablespoons flour	1 teaspoon grated lemon rind
2 tablespoons butter	1 bay leaf
	2 tablespoons minced parsley

Trim the fat off the lamb; rub the chops with a mixture of the salt, pepper, and flour. Melt the butter in a heavy skillet; brown the chops in it. Pour off the fat. Add the wine, rosemary, garlic, lemon rind, and bay leaf. Bring to a boil, cover, and cook over low heat 45 minutes, or until tender. Sprinkle with the parsley before serving.

Serves 4.

Serve with a red Bordeaux or Burgundy, a white Rhône wine, or a *rosé*.

RESTES DE GIGOT À LA BRISSAC
LEFTOVER LAMB IN WHITE WINE SAUCE

2 tablespoons butter	¾ cup dry white wine
8 slices roast lamb (leftovers)	2 tablespoons olive oil
2 tablespoons chopped onion	1 teaspoon salt
1 teaspoon chopped parsley	¼ teaspoon freshly ground black pepper
2 tablespoons flour	

Melt the butter in a skillet; brown the lamb slices in it on both sides. Add the chopped onion and parsley; sauté 5 minutes. Stir in the flour until browned. Add the wine, stirring steadily to the boiling point. Cover, and cook over medium heat 30 minutes. Add the olive oil, salt, and pepper, and cook 10 minutes longer. Taste for seasoning. Serve with boiled potatoes or boiled rice.

Serves 4.

Serve with a red Bordeaux or Burgundy, a white Rhône wine, or a *rosé*.

CASSOULET

4 cups dried white beans	1½ pounds pork, cubed
2 onions	1 pound lamb, cubed
2 cloves	1½ cups chopped onion
2 cloves garlic, minced	1 6-ounce can tomato sauce
⅛ pound salt pork, diced	1½ cups dry white wine
1 bay leaf	1 tablespoon salt
½ teaspoon thyme	2 garlic sausages
2 tablespoons salad oil	1 roast duck

Wash the beans, cover with water, and bring to a boil. Cook 2 minutes. Remove from heat and let soak 1 hour. Drain. Put in a deep pan with 2 quarts water, the onions stuck with the cloves, the garlic, salt pork, bay leaf, and thyme; bring to a boil, and cook over medium heat 1 hour.

Meanwhile, heat the oil in a skillet; brown the lamb and pork on all sides. Remove. Add the chopped onion to skillet and let brown. Mix browned meats, chopped onion, tomato sauce, wine, and salt into the pan of beans; cover, and cook over low heat 1 hour. Transfer to a large casserole. Slice the sausages and cut meat from bones of duck. Lightly mix them into the contents of casserole. Taste for seasoning, and bake in a 350° oven 40 minutes.

Serves 8-10.

Serve with a red Bordeaux or Burgundy, a red Rhône wine, or an Italian red wine like Bardolino.

ROAST LEG OF VEAL

1 leg of veal
2 teaspoons salt
½ teaspoon freshly ground
    black pepper
1 clove garlic, minced
2 onions, quartered

2 carrots, diced
⅛ teaspoon thyme
1 bay leaf
½ cup melted butter
1 cup dry white wine

Have the leg of veal boned, larded, and tied. Rub the veal with a mixture of the salt, pepper, and garlic.

Place the veal in a roasting pan, add the onions, carrots, thyme, and bay leaf. Roast in a 375° oven 20 minutes. Pour off the fat. Add the butter and wine. Reduce heat to 300° and roast 2 hours longer, or until meat is tender, basting frequently. (Or 170° on a meat thermometer). Transfer meat to a hot serving platter and skim the fat off the gravy.

Serves 6-8.

ROLLED VEAL RUMP WITH SOUR CREAM

4-pound boned rump of veal
2 cloves garlic, minced
6 anchovies, mashed
¼ teaspoon thyme
6 tablespoons butter
2 cups dry white wine
2 teaspoons salt

½ teaspoon freshly ground
    black pepper
2 tablespoons flour
¼ cup dry sherry
1 cup sour cream
2 tablespoons capers

Have the veal pounded lightly to flatten.

Lay the meat flat, with the boned surface up. Cream together the garlic, anchovies, thyme, and 2 tablespoons of butter. Spread over the meat, roll, and tie in several places. Place the veal in a glass or pottery bowl, pour the wine over it, and marinate 3 hours or more, turning and basting occasionally.

Drain and dry the meat, reserving the marinade. Rub the meat with the salt and pepper. Heat the remaining butter in a Dutch oven; brown the meat in it on all sides. Slip a rack under the meat, add the marinade, cover, and cook over low heat 2 hours, or until the meat is tender. Transfer the meat to a hot serving platter.

Blend the flour with the sherry, and stir into the gravy until thickened, then cook 2 minutes longer.

Blend in the sour cream and capers, taste for seasoning, and heat but do not let boil. Slice the meat, pour some of the gravy over it, and serve the rest separately.

Serves 8.

STUFFED VEAL CHOPS

6 rib veal chops, cut
    ¾ inch thick
	½ teaspoon freshly ground
	    black pepper

6 slices prosciutto ham	¼ cup flour
6 tablespoons cream cheese	6 tablespoons butter
1 tablespoon minced truffles	¾ cup dry white wine
2 teaspoons salt	

Have the chops cut through center right to the bone. In each, put a slice of ham, a tablespoon of cream cheese and a few pieces of truffle. Press down the cut edges firmly and fasten with toothpicks. Season with the salt and pepper; dip in flour.

Heat the butter in a skillet; sauté the veal until browned on both sides. Add the wine; cover, and cook over low heat 20 minutes, or until tender, turning the chops once or twice.

Serves 6.

Serve with any dry light red wine, especially a Bordeaux.

CÔTES DE VEAU AUX HERBES
VEAL CHOPS WITH HERBS

6 veal chops, cut 1 inch thick	¼ cup chopped green onions
2 tablespoons olive oil	1 clove garlic, minced
6 tablespoons butter	½ teaspoon thyme
1½ teaspoons salt	½ teaspoon basil
½ teaspoon freshly ground black pepper	½ cup dry white wine
	¼ cup heavy cream

Rinse and dry the chops. Heat the oil and 2 tablespoons of the butter in a large skillet; brown the chops in it on both sides. Transfer to a shallow casserole and sprinkle with the salt and pepper. Pour off the fat from the skillet. Melt 2 tablespoons of the remaining butter in the skillet;

sauté the green onions 2 minutes. Add the garlic, thyme, basil, and wine. Bring to a boil, scraping the skillet for any browned particles. Pour contents of skillet over the chops. Cover, and bake in a 325° oven 30 minutes, or until chops are tender. Baste, and turn a few times.

Transfer the chops to a hot platter. Place casserole over direct heat. Stir the cream into the pan juices. Bring to a boil, and cook over high heat 2 minutes. Taste for seasoning, then stir in the remaining butter in small pieces until just melted. Pour over the chops.

Serves 6.

Serve with a light red Bordeaux or Burgundy, especially a Beaujolais, or with a rosé.

VITELLO CON PEPERONI
VEAL AND PEPPERS

4 tablespoons butter	1½ pounds tomatoes, chopped
3 pounds boneless veal, cut in ½-inch cubes	1 cup Marsala wine or sweet sherry
2 teaspoons salt	4 tablespoons olive oil
¼ teaspoon dried ground red peppers	1½ cups thinly sliced onion
½ teaspoon oregano	1 clove garlic, minced
2 tablespoons flour	4 green peppers, sliced
1 cup beef broth	

Melt the butter in a saucepan; sauté the veal, salt, red peppers, and oregano until browned, stirring frequently. Mix in the flour. Add the broth, tomatoes, and wine. Bring to a boil, cover, and cook over low heat 30 minutes, stirring occasionally.

Heat the oil in a skillet; sauté the onion slices, garlic, and green peppers 10 minutes, stirring occasionally. Then stir into the veal mixture. Cook 10 minutes longer. Taste for seasoning. Serve with macaroni or rice.

Serves 6-8.

Serve with a dry Italian red wine like Bardolino, a red Bordeaux or Burgundy, or a rosé.

ESCALOPES DE VEAU À LA SAVOYARDE
VEAL IN VERMOUTH SAUCE

1 pound veal scaloppine	4 tablespoons butter
¼ cup flour	½ cup dry vermouth
1¼ teaspoons salt	½ cup heavy cream
¼ teaspoon white pepper	

You should have about 12 pieces of veal. Be sure the veal is cut thin, then pounded. Dip the pieces lightly in a mixture of the flour, salt, and pepper.

Melt the butter in a skillet; brown the veal in it over high heat. Add the vermouth, bring to a boil, and cook a few seconds. Add the cream, shaking the pan until the mixture boils, then cook over low heat 5 minutes, turning the veal once.

Serves 4.

Serve with a dry white Burgundy, an Alsatian wine like Traminer, a dry German white wine, or a *rosé*.

OISEAX DE VEAU
VEAL BIRDS IN WINE

2 pounds leg of veal	3 tablespoons grated onion
2 teaspoons salt	2 cloves garlic, minced
½ teaspoon freshly ground black pepper	2 tablespoons minced parsley
¼ teaspoon nutmeg	4 tablespoons butter
¼ teaspoon thyme	1 cup dry white wine
¼ pound sausage meat	6 small white onions
½ teaspoon marjoram	½ pound mushrooms, sliced
	1 bay leaf

Have the butcher pound the veal as thin as possible; then cut into 6 pieces each, about 6 inches by 4 inches. Rub pieces with a mixture of 1½ teaspoons salt, ¼ teaspoon pepper, the nutmeg, and thyme.

Mix the sausage meat with the marjoram, grated onion, garlic, parsley, and remaining salt and pepper. Spread the mixture on the veal pieces and roll them up. Tie securely with bread, or fasten with skewers or toothpicks.

Melt the butter in a deep skillet; brown the veal rolls in it. Add the wine, onions, mushrooms, and bay leaf. Cover, and bake in a 375° oven 45 minutes, or until tender. Shake the casserole once or twice, but don't lift the cover. Discard the bay leaf, and taste for seasoning.

Serves 6.

Serve with a red Bordeaux or Burgundy, a dry white Burgundy, a dry German white wine, or a *rosé*.

VEAL STEW IN RED WINE

¼ pound salt pork, diced	3 tablespoons flour
3 pounds boneless veal, cut in 1½-inch cubes	2 cups dry red wine
12 small white onions	2 teaspoons finely chopped bay leaves
3 carrots, sliced	¼ teaspoon thyme
1½ teaspoons salt	½ pound mushrooms, sliced and sautéed
½ teaspoon white pepper	
1 clove garlic, minced	2 tablespoons minced parsley

Brown the salt pork in a deep skillet or casserole; remove the browned pieces and reserve. Pour off all but 3 tablespoons fat. In the fat remaining, brown the veal, onions, and carrots. Sprinkle with the salt, pepper, garlic, and flour; add the wine, bay leaves, and thyme. Cover, and cook over low heat 1¼ hours, or until the veal is tender. Skim off the fat. Add the pork bits, mushrooms, and parsley. Cook 5 minutes longer. Taste for seasoning.

Serves 6-8.

Serve with a dry red Bordeaux or Burgundy, an Italian red wine like Bardolino, or a *rosé*.

FRENCH VEAL AND BLACK OLIVES

3 pounds boneless veal, cut into 1½-inch cubes	¾ cup sliced onion
	1 clove garlic, minced
½ cup flour	½ teaspoon thyme
2½ teaspoons salt	1 cup dry white wine
½ teaspoon freshly ground black pepper	1 tablespoon tomato paste
	½ cup chicken broth
4 tablespoons butter	1 cup sliced black olives

Toss the veal in a mixture of the flour, salt, and pepper. Melt the butter in a casserole or deep skillet with ovenproof handle; brown the veal in it. Mix in the sliced onion and garlic; cook until onions brown. Add the thyme, wine, tomato paste, and broth. Cover, and bake in a 325° oven 2 hours. Add the olives, and bake 15 minutes longer. Serves 6-8.

Serve with a white Burgundy, a dry German white wine, an Alsatian wine like Traminer, or a *rosé*.

FRICADELLES DE VEAU À LA CRÈME
VEAL CROQUETTES WITH CREAM

3 slices white bread, trimmed	½ cup flour
½ cup milk	3 tablespoons vegetable oil
1 pound ground veal	4 tablespoons butter
1¼ teaspoons salt	½ cup dry white wine
½ teaspoon white pepper	1 teaspoon basil
1 egg, beaten	½ cup heavy cream
¼ cup minced parsley	

Soak the bread in the milk until very soft, then drain and mash smooth. Mix with the veal, salt, pepper, egg, and 3 tablespoons of the parsley. Shape into 8 patties, ½ inch thick. Dip in the flour.

Heat the oil and 2 tablespoons of the butter in a large skillet. Brown the patties in it on both sides. Pour off most of the fat, cover the skillet, and cook over low heat 15 minutes, turning the patties once.

Transfer patties to a hot serving platter. Pour off the fat. Add the wine and basil. Bring to a boil, scraping the bottom for any browned particles. Add the cream; cook over high heat 3 minutes. Stir in the remaining butter in small pieces until melted. Pour over the patties, and sprinkle them with the remaining parsley. Serves 4-6.

Serve with a light red Burgundy or Bordeaux, a white Burgundy, or a *rosé*.

MOUSSE AU JAMBON
HAM MOUSSE

1 envelope (tablespoon) gelatin	½ teaspoon salt
	⅛ teaspoon cayenne pepper
¼ cup cold water	2 cups finely ground boiled
1½ cups beef broth	ham
1 cup medium sherry	¾ cup heavy cream

Soften the gelatin in the water. Bring the broth to a boil; stir in the gelatin until dissolved. Mix in the sherry, salt, and cayenne pepper. Cool until mixture begins to thicken, then beat with an electric mixer or rotary beater until foamy. Mix in the ham, and taste for seasoning.

Whip the cream, and fold into the ham mixture. Turn into a lightly oiled 1½-quart mold. Chill until set. Carefully unmold onto a chilled serving dish.

Serves 4-6.

Serve with a *rosé* wine.

TRANCHES DE JAMBON AUX MADÈRE
SAUTÉED SLICED HAM IN MADEIRA

6 slices cooked ham, cut ½-inch thick	¾ cup beef broth
	2 teaspoons tomato paste
3 tablespoons butter	⅛ teaspoon freshly ground
3 tablespoons chopped green onions	black pepper
	1¼ cups heavy cream
3 tablespoons flour	3 tablespoons cognac
¾ cup Madeira or sweet sherry	

Trim the fat off the ham. Cut each slice in half cross-wise. Melt the butter in a skillet; brown the ham in it on both sides. Remove ham and keep it warm. Pour off all but 2 tablespoons of the fat. Add the chopped green onions; sauté 1 minute. Blend in the flour; cook 1 minute. Gradually add the wine and broth, stirring steadily to the boiling point. Blend in the tomato paste and pepper; cook over low heat 5 minutes. Stir in the cream, bring to a boil, and cook over low heat 5 minutes. Return ham to the skillet; cook 5 minutes, basting frequently. Heat cognac; set aflame and pour over the ham.

Serves 6.
Serve with a dry German white wine, a white Burgundy,
a dry Italian white wine like white Chianti, or a *rosé*.

JAMBON À LA CRÈME
HAM IN CREAM SAUCE

3 tablespoons butter	1 tablespoon flour
6 slices boiled ham, cut	1 cup dry white wine
½ inch thick	½ cup heavy cream

Melt the butter in a skillet. Cook the ham over low heat
for 2 minutes on each side. Sprinkle with the flour. Stir in
the wine. Cook over medium heat until the liquid is reduced to about half. Transfer the ham to a hot platter.
Stir the cream into the pan juices. Bring to a boil, and
immediately pour over the ham.
Serves 6.
Serve with a dry German white wine, a white Burgundy,
or a *rosé*.

MAIALE MARINATO
MARINATED FRESH HAM

5 pounds fresh ham	½ teaspoon freshly ground
3 cups dry red wine	black pepper
1 cup chopped onion	2 tablespoons olive oil
½ cup sliced carrot	1 cup beef broth
2 cloves garlic, minced	2 tablespoons minced
¼ teaspoon thyme	parsley
1 bay leaf	3 tablespoons capers
2 teaspoons salt	

Trim the fat off the ham, and place ham in a glass or
pottery bowl. Mix together the wine, onion, carrot, garlic,
thyme, bay leaf, salt, and pepper. Pour over the ham;
marinate overnight, basting occasionally. Drain the meat,
reserving the marinade.
Heat the oil in a Dutch oven; brown the meat in it.
Pour off the fat. Heat the marinade and pour over the
meat. Cover and roast in a 350° oven 3 hours, or until
tender. Add a little of the broth from time to time and

baste frequently. Transfer the meat to a platter. Skim the fat from the gravy and stir in the parsley and capers.

Serves 8-10.

Serve with a German white wine, or if you wish, with a *rosé*.

JAMBON AU ANANAS
HAM WITH CHAMPAGNE SAUCE AND PINEAPPLE

12-pound ham
2 beaten eggs
1 cup brown sugar
1 can sliced pineapple

1½ cups champagne or dry white wine
2 tablespoons butter

Cook the ham according to the package directions, and drain well. Score the fat in a diamond design, brush with the egg, and spread with the brown sugar. Drain the pineapple and reserve ¾ cup juice. Put ham in a roasting pan and pour the pineapple juice and champagne around it. Bake in a 375° oven 1 hour, basting frequently to glaze. Transfer ham to a hot serving platter. Skim the fat from the pan juices.

Melt the butter in a skillet, and lightly brown the pineapple slices on both sides. Arrange around the ham. Serve the gravy separately.

Serves 12-16.

Serve with champagne, a dry German white wine, a white Burgundy like Pouilly-Fuissé, or a dry Italian white wine like Orvieto.

MARINATED PORK LOIN

8-pound loin of pork
1 quart dry red wine
1 tablespoon wine vinegar
1 cup chopped onions
2 cloves garlic, minced
2 teaspoons salt

¾ teaspoon freshly ground black pepper
½ teaspoon thyme
2 bay leaves
2 tablespoons lard or butter
¼ cup orange marmalade

Have the pork boned and tied up.

Combine the wine, vinegar, chopped onion, garlic, salt, pepper, thyme, and bay leaves in a saucepan. Bring to a boil, and cook over low heat 10 minutes. Place the pork in a large glass or pottery bowl and pour the marinade over it. Marinate in the refrigerator 24-36 hours, turning the meat and basting occasionally. Remove meat, dry with paper towels, and reserve the marinade.

Heat the fat in a Dutch oven or casserole; brown the meat in it on all sides. Pour off the fat. Heat the marinade and pour half over the meat. Cover, and roast in a 350° oven 2½ hours, or until tender, basting frequently and adding more marinade as needed. Remove cover for last half-hour.

Transfer the meat to a platter. Strain the gravy into a saucepan and skim off the fat. Stir the marmalade into it, and taste for seasoning. Thicken, if necessary, with a little cornstarch or flour mixed with water.

Serves 6-8.

Serve with a *rosé* wine.

ASADO DE PUERCO
MARINATED ROAST PORK

8-pound loin of pork	½ teaspoon oregano
2½ teaspoons salt	2 cups chopped onion
1 teaspoon freshly ground black pepper	2½ cups dry red wine
3 cloves garlic, minced	3 tablespoons olive oil
	1½ tablespoons cornstarch

Rub the pork with a mixture of the salt, pepper, garlic, and oregano. Place in a large glass or pottery bowl with the chopped onion and 1½ cups wine. Marinate in the refrigerator overnight, basting occasionally.

Heat the oil in a roasting pan. Put the undrained pork into it. Roast in a 350° oven 3 hours, basting frequently. Pour off the gravy into a saucepan and skim off the fat. Mix the cornstarch with the remaining wine, and stir into the gravy. Cook over low heat, stirring constantly, until thickened; then cook 5 minutes longer.

Serves 8-10.

Serve with a *rosé* wine.

PUERCO HORNEADO
SPICED ROAST PORK

3 cloves garlic, minced
2½ teaspoons salt
1 teaspoon freshly ground
    black pepper
½ teaspoon saffron
½ teaspoon ground cumin
½ teaspoon marjoram
 6-pound loin of pork

½ cup boiling water
1 cup dry white wine
¼ cup grated onion
2 tablespoons wine vinegar
3 tablespoons minced
    parsley
¼ teaspoon dried ground
    chili peppers

Pound together the garlic, salt, pepper, saffron, cumin, and marjoram; rub into the pork. Wrap in waxed paper or foil, and refrigerate overnight.

Place the pork in a shallow roasting pan. Roast in a 425° oven 25 minutes. Pour off the fat. Reduce heat to 350°, pour the water and ½ cup of the wine over the pork, and roast 2 hours longer, basting frequently. Transfer pork to a platter; skim the fat from the pan and place pan over direct heat. Mix in the grated onion, vinegar, parsley, chili peppers, and remaining wine; bring to a boil, scraping the bottom of the pan for browned particles. Cook 2 minutes, and serve in a sauceboat.

Serves 4-6.

Serve with a white Burgundy, a dry Italian white wine like Orvieto, or a *rosé*.

RÔTI DE PORC PROVENÇALE
ROAST PORK WITH PARSLEY COATING

8-rib loin of pork
2 cloves garlic, slivered
2 teaspoons salt
½ teaspoon freshly ground
    black pepper

2 cups dry white wine
½ teaspoon thyme
¼ cup dry bread crumbs
½ cup chopped parsley

Have the butcher saw the bottom of bones at ¼-inch intervals. Insert a garlic sliver in each. Rub the pork with the salt and pepper. Place in a large glass or pottery bowl and pour the wine, mixed with the thyme, over it. Let marinate at room temperature 2 hours, basting and turning the meat several times.

Put the pork in a roasting pan, fat side up, and pour the 1 cup of marinade over it. Cover the pan with a piece of oiled aluminum foil, and roast in a 350° oven 1 hour.

Mix together the bread crumbs and parsley. Remove the foil from the pan and spread the parsley mixture over the top of the pork, pressing it in. Pour the remaining marinade into the pan. Reduce heat to 325° and roast pork 1 hour longer, basting frequently.

Serves 4-6.

Serve with a dry German white wine, a dry white Burgundy, a white Rhône wine like Hermitage Blanc, or a *rosé*.

LOMO CON JEREZ
LOIN OF PORK WITH SHERRY

4-pound loin of pork	2 tablespoons minced
2½ teaspoons salt	parsley
½ teaspoon freshly ground	2 tablespoons olive oil
black pepper	2 cups medium sherry
2 cloves garlic, minced	

Have the fat trimmed and the loin tied up. Rub with a mixture of the salt, pepper, garlic, and parsley. Let stand 2 hours.

Heat the oil in a deep skillet or Dutch oven. Brown the pork in it on all sides. Pour off the fat. Add the sherry; bake in a 350° oven 1¾ hours, or until the pork is tender. Baste frequently.

Serves 4-6.

Serve with a *rosé* wine.

BRACIOLINE DI MAIALE AL VINO
PORK CHOPS IN WINE

6 pork chops, cut 1 inch thick	½ cup dry red wine
1½ teaspoons salt	¼ cup Marsala or sweet sherry
½ teaspoon black pepper	1 clove garlic, minced
¼ cup flour	¼ cup water
3 tablespoons olive oil	1 tablespoon tomato paste

Trim the fat off the chops, and pound them slightly to flatten. Dip in a mixture of the salt, pepper, and flour. Heat the oil in a skillet; brown the chops in it, then cover skillet and cook over low heat 10 minutes on each side. Pour off the fat. Stir the wines into the skillet; cook over high heat until liquid is reduced to half. Mix in the garlic, water, and tomato paste; cook over low heat 20 minutes longer.

Serves 6.

Serve with any dry Italian red wine.

PORK CHOPS PIZZAIOLA

6 pork chops, cut 1 inch thick
2 teaspoons salt
½ teaspoon freshly ground black pepper
2 cloves garlic, minced
2 tablespoons olive oil

½ cup canned tomato sauce
½ cup dry red wine
¼ teaspoon oregano
2 green peppers, cut julienne
½ pound mushrooms, sliced
3 Italian sausages, sliced

Trim the fat off the chops and rub chops with a mixture of the salt, pepper, and garlic. Let stand 15 minutes. Heat the oil in a skillet; brown the chops on both sides. Add the tomato sauce, wine, oregano, green peppers and mushrooms. Cover, and cook over low heat 25 minutes, or until chops are tender.

Brown the sausages in another pan, drain, and add to skillet. Cook 10 minutes longer. Taste for seasoning.

Serves 6.

Serve with Beaujolais, a dry Italian red wine like Chianti, or a *rosé*.

CÔTES DE PORC AUX PRUNEAUX
PORK CHOPS WITH PRUNES

18 unsweetened prunes
1 cup port
6 pork chops, 1 inch thick
1½ teaspoons salt
¼ teaspoon freshly ground black pepper

¼ cup flour
2 tablespoons butter
2 tablespoons cognac
2 tablespoons heavy cream

Soak the prunes in hot water 15 minutes. Drain. Add the port and cook 15 minutes, or until tender but firm.

Season the chops with the salt and pepper, and dust with the flour. Melt the butter in a skillet and sauté the chops 30 minutes, or until browned and no pink remains. Transfer the chops to a hot serving platter.

Drain the prunes, reserving ½ cup liquid, and arrange them around the chops. Heat the cognac and pour into the skillet; set aflame. When flames die, add the prune liquid and cream; cook over high heat 1 minute, scraping bottom of pan for browned particles. Pour over the chops.

Serves 6.

Serve with a dry German white wine, a white Burgundy, or a rosé.

PORK CHOPS WITH OLIVES

6 pork chops, cut 1 inch thick	1 cup sliced onion
⅓ cup flour	2 cloves garlic, minced
2½ teaspoons salt	2 cups chopped tomatoes
¾ teaspoon freshly ground black pepper	¾ cup dry white wine
2 tablespoons olive oil	2 hard-cooked eggs, chopped
	½ cup sliced black olives

Trim the fat off the chops; dip in a mixture of the flour, 1½ teaspoons of the salt, and ½ teaspoon pepper. Heat the oil in a skillet; brown the chops in it. Remove the chops. In the oil remaining in the skillet, sauté the onion slices and garlic 10 minutes. Add the tomatoes and remaining salt and pepper. Cook over low heat 10 minutes. Stir in the wine, and return the chops to skillet. Baste a few times. Cover, and bake in a 375° oven 45 minutes, or until the chops are tender. Remove cover for last 10 minutes. Sprinkle with the eggs and olives.

Serves 6.

Serve with a dry German white wine, a white Burgundy, any dry Italian white wine like Soave, or a rosé.

PORK CHOPS AND APPLES

6 pork chops, cut 1 inch thick	12 small white onions
1½ teaspoons salt	¼ cup seedless raisins
¼ teaspoon freshly ground black pepper	1 cup dry white wine
	2 tablespoons sweet sherry
4 apples, peeled and quartered	3 tablespoons brown sugar
	⅛ teaspoon thyme
	¼ teaspoon nutmeg

Season the chops with the salt and pepper. Brown the chops for 5 minutes on each side, and drain. Arrange in a casserole or baking dish with the apples, onions, and raisins over them. Add the white wine, sherry, brown sugar, thyme, and nutmeg. Cover, and bake in a 375° oven 1¼ hours, removing the cover for the last 15 minutes. Taste for seasoning.

Serves 6.

Serve with a dry German white wine, or a white Burgundy.

SPEZZATO DI MAIALE
MINCED PORK AND ONIONS

3 tablespoons butter	¼ teaspoon freshly ground black pepper
4 cups chopped onion	
1½ teaspoons salt	1 cup dry white wine
2 pounds pork, cut in ⅛-inch dice	1 tablespoon flour
	¾ cup beef broth

Melt 2 tablespoons of the butter in a skillet; mix in the chopped onion and half the salt. Cook over low heat 20 minutes, stirring frequently. Spread half the chopped onion on the bottom of a baking dish. Season the pork with the pepper and remaining salt. Spread over the onion, and cover with the remaining onion. Pour the wine into the dish.

Melt the remaining butter in a saucepan; blend in the flour. Gradually add the broth, stirring steadily to the boiling point. Cook over low heat 5 minutes, then pour over the onion. Bake in a 350° oven 1¼ hours. Serve with boiled potatoes.

Serves 4-6.

Serve with a dry German white wine, or a chilled *rosé*.

RÔTI DE PORC PÔELÉ
ROAST PORK CASSEROLE

4-pound boned rolled
   loin of pork
1 tablespoon salt
½ cup wine vinegar
1 cup dry white wine
¼ cup olive oil
2 cloves garlic, split
½ cup sliced onion

½ cup sliced carrot
8 peppercorns
1 teaspoon thyme
2 bay leaves
3 tablespoons vegetable oil
½ cup sliced green onions
½ cup beef broth

Have the pork tied. Rub the meat with the salt. In a glass or pottery bowl, combine the vinegar, wine, olive oil, garlic, onion, carrot, peppercorns, thyme, and bay leaves. Marinate the pork in the mixture 24-36 hours in the refrigerator, basting and turning the meat frequently. Drain the meat, and dry with paper towels.

Heat the vegetable oil in a casserole; brown the pork in it on all sides. Pour off all but 2 tablespoons of the fat. Add the green onions; cover, and bake in a 325° oven 2¼ hours, basting and turning meat a few times.

Transfer meat to a hot serving platter. Place casserole over direct low heat. Add the broth to the casserole; bring to a boil, and cook over high heat 3 minutes. Skim off the fat, and serve broth in a sauceboat.

Serves 8.

Serve with a dry German white wine, a white Rhône wine like Hermitage Blanc, a white Burgundy, or a *rosé*.

CHOUCROUTE À L'ALSACIENNE
SAUERKRAUT CASSEROLE

4 slices salt pork
2 cloves
1 onion
2 pounds sauerkraut
2 cloves garlic, minced
½ teaspoon freshly ground
   black pepper

3 cups dry white wine
6 pork chops
1½ teaspoons salt
6 knockwurst (thick
   frankfurters)

Cook the salt pork in boiling water 10 minutes. Drain well and dry. Place the salt pork on the bottom of a casserole. Stick the cloves in the onion and add to the casserole with the sauerkraut, garlic, pepper, and wine. Cover, and cook over low heat 2 hours. Brown the pork chops in a skillet; season with the salt, and add to the sauerkraut. Recover, and cook 1 hour. Add the knockwurst; cook 15 minutes longer.

Serves 6.

TOURTE LORRAINE
MEAT PIE, LORRAINE STYLE

1 clove garlic, minced
¼ cup chopped onion
1 tablespoon chopped parsley
1 cup dry white wine
1¾ teaspoons salt
¼ teaspoon freshly ground black pepper

1 pound lean pork, cut in ½-inch dice
1 pound veal, cut in ½-inch dice
Pastry for 2-crust pie
3 eggs, beaten
2 cups cream

In a glass or pottery bowl, mix together the garlic, onion, parsley, wine, 1½ teaspoons of the salt, and pepper; marinate the pork and veal in the mixture 24 hours in the refrigerator. Line an 11-inch, deep pie plate with half the pastry. Drain the meats and dry well, then put in the lined pie plate. Cover with the remaining pastry, and seal the edges. Cut a small hole in the center of the pastry. Bake the pie in a preheated 425° oven 25 minutes.

Beat together the eggs, cream, and remaining salt. Insert a small funnel in the hole in the pie crust and pour in the egg-cream mixture very slowly. Reduce heat to 325°, and bake 20 minutes longer. Serve hot.

Serves 6-8.

Serve with a red Burgundy or Bordeaux.

PORK AND SAUSAGES IN WINE

6 pork chops, cut 1 inch
　　thick
1½ teaspoons salt
½ teaspoon freshly ground
　　black pepper
3 slices bacon, cut in small
　　pieces
1 cup thinly sliced onion

1 cup diced carrots
1 tablespoon flour
1½ cups dry white wine
1 bay leaf
½ pound spicy sausages,
　　sliced (Italian or
　　Spanish)

Season the pork chops with the salt and pepper. Lightly brown the bacon in a deep skillet; pour off the fat. Add the onion slices and carrots; sauté 5 minutes. Arrange the chops in the pan; brown lightly on both sides. Sprinkle with the flour, and add the wine and bay leaf; cover, and cook over low heat 45 minutes. Add the sausages, re-cover, and cook 30 minutes longer, or until the pork is tender. Skim off the fat.

Serves 6.

Serve with a dry German white wine, a white Burgundy, or a *rosé*.

HAWAIIAN-CHINESE SPARERIBS

½ cup soy sauce
½ cup ketchup
½ cup dry sherry
¾ cup brown sugar
1 teaspoon salt

1 clove garlic, minced
½-inch piece ginger root,
　　crushed, or 1 teaspoon
　　powdered ginger
1 rack of spareribs

Mix the soy sauce, ketchup, sherry, sugar, salt, garlic, and ginger. Rub into the spareribs very well, then let spareribs marinate for 3 hours. Remove spareribs and place on a rack, with a shallow pan under it. Cover the bottom of the pan with ½ inch of water. Roast in a 350° oven 45 minutes, or until spareribs are browned and tender. Baste with marinade, and turn spareribs frequently. Cut into individual ribs, and serve with Chinese mustard and Chinese *duk* sauce for dunking.

Serves 6-8 as an appetizer or first course.

GLAZED TONGUE CASSEROLE

5-pound fresh beef tongue	3 cups dry white wine
2 cloves	3 tablespoons honey
1 onion	1 teaspoon cinnamon
1 bay leaf	4 thin slices lemon
6 peppercorns	

Wash the tongue, and place in a saucepan with water to cover. Add the cloves, onion, bay leaf, and peppercorns. Bring to a boil, cover, and cook over low heat 3 hours. Drain, and cool 30 minutes. Peel off the skin, and cut away the roots. Cut the tongue in 1/4-inch slices.

Arrange the sliced tongue in a casserole; add a mixture of the wine, honey, cinnamon, and lemon slices. Cover, and bake in a 375° oven 30 minutes, or until liquid is almost absorbed.

Serves 6-8.

Serve with a red Bordeaux, or a red Rhône wine.

TONGUE WITH MUSHROOM-WINE SAUCE

5-pound smoked tongue	2 tablespoons flour
2 cloves garlic, minced	1 1/2 cups dry red wine
3 tablespoons butter	1 tablespoon minced
3/4 cup chopped onion	parsley
2 cups chopped mushrooms	

Wash the tongue, cover with water, and bring to a boil. Drain; then add fresh boiling water to cover, and the garlic. Cover, and cook over low heat 2 1/2 hours, or until tongue is tender. Drain, reserving 1 1/2 cups stock. Remove the skin, and cut away the roots of the tongue.

Melt the butter in a saucepan; sauté the onion 5 minutes. Add the mushrooms; sauté 5 minutes. Blend in the flour until browned. Gradually add the wine and the reserved stock, stirring steadily to the boiling point. Cook over low heat 10 minutes. Stir in the parsley. Slice the tongue, and serve with the sauce.

Serves 8-10.

Serve with a red Bordeaux, or with a red Rhône like Hermitage or Châteauneuf-du-Pape.

TONGUE IN OLIVE SAUCE

5-pound pickled tongue
1 onion
1 stalk celery
3 tablespoons butter
1 cup chopped onion
1 clove garlic, minced
1 cup dry white wine
2 tablespoons flour
½ cup canned tomato sauce
3 tablespoons lemon juice
2 teaspoons sugar
½ teaspoon freshly ground
    black pepper
½ teaspoon powdered ginger
1 teaspoon finely chopped
    bay leaf
1 cup sliced black olives

Cook the tongue, the onion, and celery in water to cover, 3 hours, or until tender, adding boiling water from time to time to keep covered. Drain, reserving 1 cup stock. Skin the tongue, and remove roots.

Melt the butter in a saucepan; sauté the chopped onion and garlic 10 minutes. Blend in the flour until browned; gradually add the combined stock, wine, and tomato sauce, stirring constantly to the boiling point. Mix in the lemon juice, sugar, pepper, ginger, bay leaf, and olives. Cook over low heat 5 minutes. Slice the tongue, and heat in the sauce for 10 minutes. Taste for seasoning.

Serves 8-10.

Serve with a red Rhône wine like Châteauneuf-du-Pape, or a light red Bordeaux.

CASSEROLE OF VENISON

3 pounds venison, cut into
    1½-inch cubes
¼ cup flour
2 teaspoons salt
¼ teaspoon freshly ground
    black pepper
3 tablespoons vegetable oil
1 cup chopped onion
2 cloves garlic, minced
1 teaspoon paprika
2 cups dry red wine
½ cup water
1 tablespoon tomato paste
1 cup sour cream

Toss the venison in a mixture of the flour, salt, and pepper. Heat the oil in a casserole; brown the meat in it. Add the onion and garlic; cook 10 minutes, stirring frequently. Blend in the paprika, then the wine, water, and tomato paste. Bring to a boil, cover, and cook over low heat 2½ hours, or until meat is tender. Watch carefully, and add a little boiling water if necessary. Just before serving, stir the sour cream into the gravy. Heat, but do not let boil.

Serves 6-8.

Serve with a red Burgundy, a red Rhône wine like Hermitage, or an Italian red wine like Bardolino.

SAUSAGE-MEAT LOAF

¾ pound sausage meat	½ teaspoon freshly ground
1½ pounds ground beef	black pepper
2 tablespoons grated onion	½ teaspoon oregano
1 clove garlic, minced	2 tablespoons minced
2 eggs, beaten	parsley
1½ teaspoons salt	¼ cup flour
	1 cup dry red wine

Mix the sausage meat with the other ingredients except the flour and wine. Shape into a loaf, and sprinkle with the flour; place in a greased pan. Add the wine. Bake in a 350° oven 1 hour, basting frequently. Serve hot or cold.

Serves 8-10.

Serve with a red Bordeaux or Burgundy.

FOIE DE VEAU AU VIN ROUGE
CALF'S LIVER IN RED WINE

4 tablespoons butter	1½ teaspoons salt
2½ pounds calf's liver	¼ teaspoon freshly ground
(one piece)	black pepper
1 cup sliced onion	2 tablespoons minced
2 carrots, sliced	parsley
1 clove garlic, minced	2 cups dry red wine
1 bay leaf	1 cup beef broth
½ teaspoon thyme	2 tablespoons flour

Melt the butter in a casserole; brown the liver in it on both sides. Add the sliced onion, carrots, and garlic; sauté until lightly browned. Add the bay leaf, thyme, salt, pepper, parsley, 1¾ cups wine, and the broth. Cover, and bake in a 375° oven 2 hours. Turn liver occasionally. Place casserole over direct heat; mix the flour and remaining wine together, and stir into gravy until thickened. Cook

over low heat 10 minutes. Slice the liver and serve with
the gravy.

Serves 6-8.

Serve with a dry red Bordeaux or Burgundy, especially
a Beaujolais, or a dry Italian red wine like Barolo.

FEGATO DI VITELLO AL MARSALA
CALF'S LIVER IN MARSALA

1 pound calf's liver, sliced
⅛ inch thick
2 tablespoons lemon juice
⅓ cup flour
1¼ teaspoons salt

¼ teaspoon white pepper
4 tablespoons butter
⅓ cup Marsala or sweet
   sherry

Wash and dry the liver; rub with the lemon juice, then
dip in the flour mixed with the salt and pepper. Melt the
butter in a skillet; fry the liver over high heat 1 minute
on each side. Stir the wine into the pan; cook over low
heat 2 minutes, basting almost constantly.

Serves 4.

Serve with a dry red Bordeaux or Burgundy, especially
a Beaujolais, or with a dry Italian red wine like Valpolicella.

FEGATO DI VITELLO ALLA VENEZIANA
CALF'S LIVER, WITH ONIONS AND WINE

1 pound calf's liver
¼ pound butter
1½ cups thinly sliced onion
1 teaspoon salt

¼ teaspoon freshly ground
   black pepper
¼ cup dry white wine
2 tablespoons minced
   parsley

Cut the liver in paper-thin slices, and then into strips
about 1 inch by 2 inches.

Melt the butter in a skillet; add the onion slices. Cover,
and cook the onions over very low heat 15 minutes, or
until lightly browned and soft. Add the liver, and cook
over high heat 3 minutes, stirring almost constantly. Season with the salt and pepper. Transfer to a hot platter. Stir
the wine and parsley into the skillet; bring to a boil and
pour over the liver.

Serves 4.

Serve with a dry red Bordeaux or Burgundy, or a dry
Italian red wine like Valpolicella.

RIS DE VEAU LUCULLUS
CREAMED SWEETBREADS AND MUSHROOMS, LUCULLUS

3 pairs parboiled
   sweetbreads
6 tablespoons butter
1 cup port
1 pound mushrooms, sliced

2 teaspoons beef extract
1 teaspoon salt
¼ teaspoon freshly ground
   white pepper
2 cups heavy cream

Cut the parboiled sweetbreads in four. Heat 4 tablespoons butter in a casserole; lightly brown the sweetbreads
in it. Add the port; cook over low heat until reduced to
half. Melt the remaining butter in a skillet; sauté the
mushrooms 5 minutes. Mix into the casserole with the beef
extract, salt, pepper, and cream. Cover, and bake in a 350°
oven 20 minutes. Thicken sauce, if necessary, with 1 tablespoon flour kneaded with 1 tablespoon butter.

Serves 6.

Serve with a white Burgundy or Bordeaux, a dry German white wine, or a *rosé*.

SAUTÉED SWEETBREADS WITH MUSHROOMS

2 pair parboiled
   sweetbreads
¼ cup flour
3 tablespoons butter
1 teaspoon salt
¼ teaspoon white pepper
2 tablespoons warmed
   cognac

¾ cup dry white wine
¼ cup chicken broth
½ teaspoon tomato paste
1 clove garlic, minced
8 mushroom caps, sautéed
2 tablespoons minced
   parsley

Cut the sweetbreads in half lengthwise, so as to make
them half as thick. Dip them in the flour (reserve 1 tablespoon). Melt the butter in a skillet; brown the sweetbreads
on both sides. Season with the salt and pepper. Pour the
warmed cognac over them and set aflame. Remove sweetbreads from skillet and keep warm. Blend the reserved
flour into the pan. Add the wine, broth, tomato paste, and

garlic, stirring steadily to the boiling point; cook over low heat 5 minutes. Place the sweetbreads on toast or sautéed bread slices, with a mushroom on top of each. Pour the sauce over all, and sprinkle with the parsley.

Serves 8, as a first course, or 4 as a main course.

Serve with a dry white Burgundy, a dry German white wine, or an Italian white wine like Orvieto or white Chianti.

RIS DE VEAU AU VIN BLANC
SWEETBREADS IN WHITE WINE

4 pair sweetbreads	1½ teaspoons salt
1 tablespoon vinegar	¼ teaspoon white pepper
3 cups water	2 tablespoons sweet sherry
3 tablespoons butter	1 cup dry white wine
1½ cups sliced onion	½ cup chicken broth
1 cup grated carrot	2 cups fresh or frozen
3 tablespoons minced	green peas
parsley	¾ cup chopped mushrooms
1 bay leaf	

Wash the sweetbreads and soak in ice water for 2 hours; drain, and combine in a saucepan with the vinegar and water. Bring to a boil, and cook over low heat 10 minutes. Drain, cover with cold water, and let cool. Drain. Remove membranes and tubes, and cut each sweetbread in quarters.

Melt the butter in a casserole; sauté the onion slices and grated carrot for 10 minutes, stirring frequently. Arrange the sweetbreads over them and add the parsley, bay leaf, salt, pepper, sherry, white wine, broth, peas, and mushrooms. Bake in a 375° oven 1 hour, turning the sweetbreads once or twice. Discard bay leaf.

Serves 6-8.

Serve with a white Burgundy, a dry German white wine, or a Loire Valley white wine like Pouilly-Fumé.

SWEETBREADS, HAM, AND MUSHROOMS

3 pair sweetbreads
1 tablespoon vinegar
2 teaspoons salt
¼ cup flour
4 tablespoons olive oil
4 tablespoons butter

¼ teaspoon white pepper
1 cup sliced sautéed
   mushrooms
½ cup julienne-cut
   cooked ham
¾ cup dry white wine

Wash the sweetbreads, cover with cold water, and let soak 1 hour. Drain, add fresh water to cover, the vinegar, and 1 teaspoon salt. Bring to a boil, and cook over low heat 5 minutes. Drain, cover with cold water, and let stand 20 minutes. Drain, remove the membranes and tubes, but leave the sweetbreads whole. Dry, then dip lightly in the flour.

Heat the oil in a skillet; brown the sweetbreads in it. Pour off the oil. Add the butter, pepper, mushrooms, ham, wine, and the remaining salt. Bring to a boil and cook over low heat 10 minutes.

Serves 6.

Serve with a white Burgundy, a dry German white wine, or a dry white Bordeaux.

RIS DE VEAU AU MARRONS
SWEETBREADS WITH CHESTNUTS AND MUSHROOMS

6 pair sweetbreads
1 tablespoon vinegar
2 teaspoons salt
6 tablespoons butter
1 cup chopped onion
¾ cup grated carrot
½ cup chopped celery
½ cup dry white wine

½ cup Madeira wine
¾ cup chicken broth
¼ teaspoon freshly ground
   black pepper
½ cup diced ham
¾ cup sliced mushrooms
½ cup coarsely chopped
   cooked chestnuts

Soak the sweetbreads in cold water for 2 hours in the refrigerator. Drain, and cover with fresh water. Add the vinegar and salt. Bring to a boil, and cook 5 minutes. Drain, and remove the membranes. Place a weight on the sweetbreads (a breadboard or a plate) and chill.

Melt 3 tablespoons butter in a skillet; sauté the onion, carrot, and celery for 10 minutes. Add the white wine and

Madeira. Arrange the sweetbreads in the skillet and add enough of the broth to half cover them. Season with the pepper. Cover, and bake in a 350° oven 30 minutes.

In a separate skillet, melt remaining butter. Sauté the ham, mushrooms, and chestnuts in it for 5 minutes. Add to the sweetbreads, and taste for seasoning.

Serves 6.

QUEUE DE BOEUF
BRAISED OXTAILS IN RED WINE

2 oxtails	3 cups dry red wine
½ cup flour	3 cups water
3 slices salt pork, diced	2 teaspoons tomato paste
1 cup diced onion	3 potatoes, peeled and
1 carrot, grated	quartered
1 teaspoon salt	2 cups fresh or frozen
½ teaspoon freshly ground	green peas
black pepper	

Have the oxtails cut in 1-inch pieces. Cover with boiling water, drain, and dry. Roll in the flour. Brown the salt pork in a Dutch oven or casserole; drain off all but 2 table-spoons fat. Add the oxtails, onion, and grated carrot, and cook until browned. Mix in the salt, pepper, and 2 cups wine. Cook over high heat until wine evaporates. Add the water, tomato paste, and remaining wine; cover, and cook over low heat 3 hours. Add potatoes and peas; cook 30 minutes longer. Taste for seasoning.

Serves 6.

Serve with a dry red Bordeaux, a Burgundy like Beaujolais, or a red Rhône wine like Châteauneuf-du-Pape.

RAGOUT DE QUEUE DE BOEUF
OXTAIL STEW

2 2-pound oxtails, cut in
    serving-size pieces
¾ cup flour
2 teaspoons salt
½ teaspoon freshly ground
    black pepper
½ teaspoon thyme
4 tablespoons olive oil
2 cups boiling water
3 cups dry red wine
2 cloves

12 small white onions
3 sprigs parsley ⎫ tied
2 stalks celery ⎬ together
1 bay leaf ⎭ (bouquet garni)
1 clove garlic, minced
1 leek
3 carrots, cut in eighths
    lengthwise
4 potatoes, peeled and diced
1 cup sliced mushrooms

Pour boiling water over the oxtail pieces; drain and dry.
Roll in a mixture of the flour, salt, pepper, and thyme.
Heat the oil in a deep heavy casserole or Dutch oven, and
brown the oxtails on all sides. Pour off the fat. Add the
boiling water and wine. Stick the cloves in one of the
onions. Add to the casserole with other onions, the bouquet
garni, the garlic, and leek. Cover tightly, and bake in a
300° oven 2½ hours. Add the carrots, potatoes, and mushrooms. Re-cover, and bake 1 hour longer. Skim fat off the
top; taste for seasoning.

Serves 6-8.
Serve with a red Bordeaux or Burgundy.

TRIPPA ALLA FIORENTINA
TRIPE IN MEAT SAUCE

2 pounds tripe
2 tablespoons butter
¾ cup chopped onion
½ cup grated carrot
½ pound beef (one piece)
¾ cup dry white wine
¾ cup peeled, chopped
    tomatoes

2 teaspoons salt
½ teaspoon freshly ground
    black pepper
½ teaspoon thyme
½ cut grated Parmesan
    cheese

Wash the tripe, cover with water, and bring to a boil;
cook over low heat 1 hour. Drain, cool, and cut into strips

2 inches long and ½ inch wide. Meanwhile prepare the sauce.

Melt the butter in a saucepan; brown the onion, carrot, and beef in it. Add the wine, tomatoes, salt, and pepper; bring to a boil, cover, and cook over low heat 1 hour. Add the thyme and tripe; re-cover, and cook 1 hour longer. Remove the beef. Serve sprinkled with the cheese.

Serves 6-8.

Serve with a dry German white wine, a light red Bordeaux, or a *rosé*.

CALF'S FOOT STEW

4 calf's feet	1 tablespoon salt
3 quarts water	½ teaspoon freshly ground
1 cup sliced onion	black pepper
3 sprigs parsley	1 cup chopped tomatoes
2 stalks celery	1½ cups dry red wine
1 bay leaf	2 egg yolks

Have the feet chopped up, bone and all, into small pieces. Pour boiling water over them, and scrape the skin. Combine the feet with the water, onion slices, parsley, celery, bay leaf, salt, pepper, and tomatoes. Bring to a boil, and cook over low heat 3 hours. Remove the feet; cut the meat in small pieces, discarding the bones. Mix the wine into the stock; cook over high heat 20 minutes. Return the meat; cook 10 minutes. Beat the egg yolks in a bowl; gradually add the hot mixture, stirring steadily to prevent curdling. Serve in deep bowls, with garlic toast.

Serves 6-8.

Serve with any dry red wine, especially a Burgundy.

BRAISED KIDNEYS

1 pound veal kidneys	1 teaspoon grated lemon
3 cups boiling water	rind
2 tablespoons lemon juice	½ cup Marsala or sweet
4 tablespoons butter	sherry
1¼ teaspoons salt	3 tablespoons minced
¼ teaspoon freshly ground	parsley
black pepper	

Wash the kidneys, cut in half, and remove the core. Soak in the boiling water mixed with the lemon juice for 3 minutes. Drain, then slice thin.

Melt the butter in a skillet; sauté the kidneys 5 minutes. Mix in the salt, pepper, lemon rind, and wine. Cook over medium heat 5 minutes. Sprinkle with the parsley.

Serves 4.

Serve with a dry red Bordeaux or a Burgundy, especially a Beaujolais, or a dry Italian red wine like Valpolicella.

HASSENPFEFFER
MARINATED RABBIT

2 rabbits (about 4 pounds)	1 tablespoon pickling spice
2 cups dry red wine	3 bay leaves
1 cup wine vinegar	2 cups sliced onions
1 cup water	½ cup flour
2 teaspoons salt	4 tablespoons butter
¾ teaspoon freshly ground	1 tablespoon sugar
black pepper	1 cup sour cream
6 cloves	

Rabbits are available fresh and frozen. Have the rabbits cut in serving-size pieces. If frozen rabbits are used, thaw them partially. Place in pieces in a large glass or pottery bowl. Add a mixture of the wine, vinegar, water, salt, pepper, cloves, pickling spice, bay leaves, and onion slices. Cover, and let marinate in the refrigerator 36 hours, basting and turning the pieces a few times.

Drain and dry the rabbit pieces. Reserve the marinade. Roll the rabbit in the flour. Melt the butter in a casserole; brown the rabbit pieces in it. Strain the marinade over the rabbit, and add the sugar. Bring to a boil; cover, and cook over low heat 45 minutes, or until tender. Taste for seasoning. If gravy is thin, stir 2 tablespoons flour, mixed with a little water, into the gravy, then gradually mix in the sour cream. Heat, but do not let boil.

Serves 6.

Serve with a heavy Burgundy, especially a Beaujolais, or a red Rhône wine like Châteauneuf-du-Pape.

Vegetables

CARCIOFI ALLA ROMANA
ROMAN-STYLE ARTICHOKES

6 small artichokes	2 teaspoons salt
2 cloves garlic, minced	½ teaspoon freshly ground
1 cup minced parsley	black pepper
1 teaspoon fresh mint,	¼ cup olive oil
chopped, or ⅛	1 cup dry white wine
teaspoon dried	½ cup chicken broth

Remove the tough outer leaves of the artichokes; cut off the sharp points of the remaining leaves. Carefully force the centers apart and cut out the chokes (furry centers). Mix together the garlic, parsley, mint, 1 teaspoon salt, and ¼ teaspoon pepper. Stuff the centers of the artichokes. Arrange close together in a casserole; sprinkle with the oil. Cook over medium heat 10 minutes. Add the wine, broth, and remaining salt and pepper. Cover, and cook over medium heat 45 minutes, or until artichokes are tender.

Serves 6.

JERUSALEM ARTICHOKES IN WHITE WINE

1½ pounds Jerusalem	1 clove garlic, minced
artichokes	¾ cup dry white wine
6 tablespoons butter	1 teaspoon salt
½ cup chopped onion	⅛ teaspoon white pepper

Scrub the artichokes, pare, and dice. Melt the butter in a skillet; sauté the onion and garlic 5 minutes. Add the diced artichokes; sauté until lightly browned. Mix in the wine, salt, and pepper. Cover, and cook over low heat 15 minutes, or until tender.

Serves 4-6.

HARICOTS VERTS PORTUGAISE
GREEN BEANS, PORTUGUESE STYLE

2 slices salt pork or
    bacon, diced
1 cup peeled, chopped
    tomatoes
1½ pounds green beans, or
    2 packages frozen
    beans, thawed

½ cup dry white wine
¼ cup beef broth
1 teaspoon salt
⅛ teaspoon white pepper
2 tablespoons minced
    parsley

Lightly brown the salt pork in a saucepan; pour off the fat. Add the tomatoes, beans, wine, broth, salt, and pepper. Bring to a boil; cover, and cook over low heat 30 minutes. Drain off most of the liquid. Taste for seasoning. Sprinkle with the parsley and serve.

Serves 6.

BAKED BEANS IN WINE

3 cups dried white beans
1½ teaspoons salt
½ pound salt pork
2 onions
4 cloves
2 cups dry white wine

⅓ cup dark rum
¾ cup molasses
2 teaspoons dry mustard
½ teaspoon crushed dried
    red peppers

Wash the beans, cover with water, bring to a boil, and let soak 1 hour. Drain, add fresh water to cover, and the salt; bring to a boil, and cook over low heat 35 minutes. Drain.

Cut the salt pork into ½-inch cubes. Pour boiling water over it, and let soak 30 minutes. Drain.

Using an earthenware casserole, spread half the beans on the bottom. Cover with half the salt pork, the onions stuck with the cloves, then the remaining beans, and finally the remaining salt pork. Add a mixture of the wine, rum, molasses, mustard, and red peppers. Add enough boiling water to barely cover the beans. Cover casserole tightly and bake in a 250° oven 4½ hours, or until beans are tender, removing the cover for the last half-hour. Add a little boiling water from time to time during the first 4 hours to keep beans moist, but don't add any during the last half hour.

Serves 6-8.

LIMA BEANS IN WINE SAUCE

2 packages frozen lima
    beans
½ cup sour cream
¾ cup dry white wine

⅛ teaspoon white pepper
¼ cup minced pimientos
2 tablespoons minced
    parsley

Cook the lima beans ½ minute less than package directs. Drain well. Mix together the sour cream, wine, and pepper. Add to the beans, with the pimientos. Cook over low heat 5 minutes, but do not let boil. Taste for seasoning. Sprinkle with the parsley and serve.

Serves 4-6.

LIMA BEANS AND ONION CASSEROLE

4 tablespoons butter
18 small white onions, peeled
1 tablespoon flour
1 cup dry white wine
1 bay leaf
⅛ teaspoon thyme

1 teaspoon salt
⅛ teaspoon white pepper
2 cups shelled fresh lima
    beans, or 1 package
    frozen beans, thawed

Melt the butter in a casserole; sauté the onions until delicately browned. Stir in the flour and add the wine, bay leaf, thyme, salt, and pepper. Cover, and cook over low heat 15 minutes. Mix in the lima beans; cover, and cook over low heat 15 minutes, or until beans are tender. Shake the casserole occasionally to prevent burning. Taste for seasoning.

Serves 4-6.

RED CABBAGE AND APPLES IN RED WINE

2 2-pound firm heads red
    cabbage
4 tablespoons butter
4 tart apples, peeled and
    quartered
½ cup chopped onion
1½ teaspoons salt

¼ teaspoon freshly ground
    pepper
2 cloves
1 bay leaf
2 tablespoons wine vinegar
1½ cups dry red wine
2 tablespoons brown sugar

Wash cabbage, dry, and slice very thin, discarding the thick center core. Melt 2 tablespoons of the butter in a Dutch oven or heavy saucepan. Add the cabbage, apples, chopped onion, salt, pepper, cloves, bay leaf, vinegar, and red wine. Bring to a boil, cover, and cook over low heat 3 hours, adding a little hot water during cooking, if necessary. Stir in the brown sugar and remaining butter; cook 5 minutes. Remove bay leaf and cloves.

Serves 6-8.

CHOU AU CHAMPAGNE
CABBAGE IN CHAMPAGNE

3 tablespoons butter	¾ cup champagne or dry
1 cup chopped onion	white wine
1 3-pound head cabbage,	3 tomatoes, cut in eighths
shredded	1½ teaspoons salt
2 tablespoons flour	⅛ teaspoon pepper
	1 teaspoon sugar

Melt the butter in a saucepan; sauté the chopped onion and the cabbage 15 minutes, stirring frequently. Mix in the flour. Add the champagne, stirring constantly to the boiling point. Add the tomatoes, salt, pepper, and sugar. Cover, and cook over low heat 30 minutes.

Serves 6.

CABBAGE IN RED WINE

4 pounds red cabbage	3 cloves
6 tablespoons butter	1 bay leaf
3 cups diced apples	2 cups dry red wine
½ cup chopped onion	2 tablespoons vinegar
1½ teaspoons salt	3 tablespoons currant jelly

Shred the cabbage very fine. Melt the butter in a casserole or heavy saucepan. Add the cabbage, apples, onion, salt, cloves, and bay leaf. Mix lightly, then add the wine, vinegar, and jelly. Bring to a boil, cover, and cook over low heat 2½ hours. Stir once or twice, and watch carefully to prevent burning. Discard bay leaf.

Serves 6-8.

CHOUX-FLEURS BOURGUIGNON
CAULIFLOWER IN WINE SAUCE

3 tablespoons butter
1 tablespoon flour
1 teaspoon salt
1/8 teaspoon white pepper

1/2 cup dry white wine
1/2 cup heavy cream
1 medium cauliflower,
    cooked and drained

Melt the butter in a saucepan; stir in the flour, salt, and pepper. Add a mixture of the wine and cream, stirring steadily to the boiling point, then cook over low heat 5 minutes.

Place the cauliflower in a hot serving dish, and pour the sauce over it.

Serves 4-6.

CELERY WITH CHAMPAGNE SAUCE

4 tablespoons butter
3/4 cup chopped onion
1 carrot, diced
1/4 pound ham, diced
1/4 pound tongue, diced
2 tablespoons chopped
    parsley

1/2 teaspoon tarragon
1 bay leaf
3/4 cup champagne or dry
    white wine
1/2 cup chicken broth
3 bunches celery

Melt the butter in a saucepan; add the onion, carrot, ham, tongue, parsley, tarragon, bay leaf, champagne, and broth. Bring to a boil, cover, and cook over low heat 45 minutes.

Cut the leaves from the celery and remove the large outer stalks. Cut each bunch in half lengthwise. Add to the sauce; cover, and cook over low heat 15 minutes longer, or until the celery is tender. Taste for seasoning, and serve.

Serves 6.

MUSHROOMS AND ARTICHOKES

4 tablespoons butter
2 packages frozen artichoke
    hearts, thawed
1 pound mushrooms, sliced
1 1/4 teaspoons salt

1/4 teaspoon freshly ground
    black pepper
1/4 teaspoon thyme
1/2 cup dry sherry

Melt the butter in a skillet; sauté the artichoke hearts 3 minutes. Add the mushrooms; sauté 2 minutes. Season with the salt, pepper, and thyme; add the sherry. Cook over high heat 5 minutes.

Serves 6-8.

MUSHROOMS WITH FOIE GRAS

1 pound firm large white mushrooms
1 cup boiling water
¾ teaspoon salt
2 teaspoons lemon juice
3 tablespoons butter

2 tablespoons chopped shallots or onion
¼ cup finely diced ham
1 cup dry white wine
Foie gras

Wash the mushrooms and remove the stems. Chop the stems. Put caps in a saucepan with the boiling water, salt, lemon juice, and half the butter. Cover, and cook 3 minutes. Drain caps, and arrange in a buttered shallow baking dish, hollow side up. Melt the remaining butter in a skillet and sauté the shallots and ham 3 minutes; add the chopped stems; continue sautéing for 3 minutes over high heat. Add the wine, and cook over low heat 20 minutes, or until the mixture is fairly dry. Fill mushroom caps with stuffing, and put a thin slice of foie gras on each. Place in 425° oven for 5 minutes.

Serves 4.

Serve with a dry red Bordeaux or Burgundy, or if you prefer, with a *rosé*.

MUSHROOMS SAUTÉED IN WINE

4 tablespoons butter
1 pound mushrooms, sliced
1 tomato, peeled and chopped
1 tablespoon chopped parsley

½ cup dry white wine
1 teaspoon salt
⅛ teaspoon freshly ground black pepper

Melt the butter in a skillet. Add the mushrooms, tomato, and parsley. Sauté 5 minutes, stirring frequently. Add the wine, salt, and pepper. Cook over high heat for 3 minutes, stirring frequently. Serve as a vegetable, or as an appetizer on toast.

Serves 2-4.

CHAMPIGNONS BOURGUIGNON
MUSHROOMS WITH WINE BUTTER

1 cup dry red wine
1 clove garlic, minced
3 tablespoons chopped
    green onion
¼ pound (1 stick) butter
½ teaspoon freshly ground
    black pepper

1 tablespoon minced parsley
24 mushroom caps
¾ teaspoon salt
4-6 slices hot buttered
    toast, trimmed

Cook the wine, garlic, and chopped onion until reduced to half. Cool. Cream the butter (reserving 2 tablespoons), then beat in the wine mixture, pepper, and parsley.

Melt the remaining butter in a skillet; sauté the mushrooms 5 minutes. Season with the salt. Arrange the mushrooms on the toast, hollow side up. Divide the wine butter among the mushroom caps. Serve at once.

Serves 4-6.

GREEN PEPPERS IN WHITE WINE

4 tablespoons olive oil
2 cups coarsely chopped
    onion
4 cups julienne-cut green
    peppers
1 cup dry white wine

1½ teaspoons salt
¼ teaspoon freshly ground
    black pepper
2 tablespoons minced
    parsley

Heat the oil in a skillet; sauté the onion 10 minutes. Add the green peppers, wine, salt, and pepper. Cook over low heat 25 minutes, or until peppers are tender. Sprinkle with the parsley.

Serves 4-6.

STUFFED GREEN PEPPERS

6 green peppers
3 tablespoons butter
½ pound mushrooms,
　　coarsely chopped
3 tablespoons grated onion
¼ pound ham, shredded
2 tablespoons tomato paste

4 tablespoons dry bread
　　crumbs
3 tablespoons olive oil
3 tablespoons flour
¼ cup beef broth
1 cup dry white wine

Cut a 1-inch slice from the stem end of the peppers. Cover the peppers with water; bring to a boil, and cook 5 minutes. Drain and cool.

Melt the butter in a skillet; sauté the mushrooms and grated onion for 5 minutes. Add the ham and 1 tablespoon of the tomato paste. Cook over low heat 5 minutes. Stir in the bread crumbs. Stuff the peppers with the mixture. Arrange the peppers, stuffed side up, in an oiled baking dish. Sprinkle the olive oil over and around them. Bake in a 400° oven for 10 minutes. Mix together the flour, broth, wine, and remaining tomato paste. Pour over the peppers. Reduce heat to 350°, and bake 45 minutes longer, basting frequently. Taste for seasoning. Serve as an appetizer, or with roast meat or poultry.

Serves 6.

Serve with a *rosé*, a dry German white wine, or a white Burgundy.

FESTIVE POTATOES

4 large potatoes, peeled and
　　sliced as thin as possible
1½ cups thinly sliced
　　onions
2 teaspoons salt
½ teaspoon freshly ground
　　black pepper

5 tablespoons butter
½ cup dry white wine
¼ cup heavy cream
2 tablespoons dry bread
　　crumbs
2 tablespoons grated
　　Parmesan cheese

In a buttered 9-inch pie plate, arrange layers of sliced potatoes and onions, sprinkling each layer with salt and pepper, and dot with half the butter. Mix together the wine and cream, and pour over the top; sprinkle with the bread crumbs and cheese, and dot with the remaining butter. Bake in a 375° oven 45 minutes, or until the potatoes are tender. Serve in pie-shaped wedges.

Serves 4-6.

CHOUCROUTE AUX CHAMPAGNE
SAUERKRAUT WITH CHAMPAGNE

2 pounds sauerkraut
3 apples, peeled and sliced
1 teaspoon salt
½ teaspoon freshly ground
　　black pepper

3 cloves
2 cups champagne
3 tablespoons butter

Wash the sauerkraut under cold running water. Drain very well.

In a buttered casserole, arrange alternate layers of sauerkraut and apples. Sprinkle with the salt and pepper, and add the cloves. Pour the champagne over it. Dot with the butter. Cover the casserole.

Bake in a 300° oven for 1½ hours, or until the sauerkraut is tender, and almost all the liquid absorbed. Especially delicious when served with roast turkey or pork.

Serves 6-8.

Serve with any dry white wine.

Sauces and Dressings

BROWN SAUCE

¼ cup minced shallots or
  onions
2 tablespoons butter
1 tablespoon flour
2 cups canned beef broth

2 teaspoons tomato paste
1 bay leaf
⅛ teaspoon freshly ground
  black pepper
⅛ teaspoon thyme

Sauté the minced shallots or onion in the butter for 5 minutes. Stir in the flour and cook over low heat, stirring frequently, until browned. Slowly mix in the broth, stirring steadily to the boiling point. Add the tomato paste, bay leaf, pepper, and thyme, and cook over low heat 20 minutes. Strain. Use as a base for other sauces, or serve on meats.

Makes about 1½ cups.

SAUCE DUXELLES
MUSHROOM SAUCE

1 tablespoon olive oil
3 tablespoons butter
¼ pound mushrooms,
  chopped fine
2 tablespoons chopped
  shallots or green onions

⅓ cup dry sherry
1½ cups Brown Sauce
  (see recipe)
1½ tablespoons tomato paste
3 tablespoons minced
  parsley

Heat the oil and 1 tablespoon butter in a saucepan; sauté the mushrooms and shallots 3 minutes. Add the sherry; cook over high heat until sherry is almost evaporated. Mix in the Brown Sauce and tomato paste. Cook over low heat 5 minutes. Taste for seasoning. Just before serving, blend in the remaining butter. Serve with chicken, veal, eggs, or *pasta*.

Makes about 2 cups.

SAUCE ROUENNAISE

4 duck livers or 8 chicken livers
3 tablespoons minced onion
1 tablespoon butter
¼ cup dry red wine
1½ cups Brown Sauce (see recipe)
1 tablespoon cognac

Wash the livers carefully, removing any discolored areas. Purée the livers in a blender; or chop, then force through a fine sieve. Refrigerate until needed.

Sauté the minced onion in the butter 5 minutes. Add the wine, and cook until reduced to half. Stir in the Brown Sauce and cognac; cook over low heat 10 minutes. Just before serving, mix ¼ cup of the hot sauce with the liver. Return to the balance of the sauce; heat, but do not let boil. This is an extremely rich sauce. Serve with duck.

Makes about 1¾ cups.

SAUCE LYONNAISE

¼ cup minced onion
2 tablespoons butter
1 cup dry white wine
1½ cups Brown Sauce

Sauté the minced onion in the butter 10 minutes. Add the wine and Brown Sauce; cook over low heat 5 minutes. Serve with game or beef.

Makes 2 cups.

BORDELAISE SAUCE

Large marrow bone
2 tablespoons minced shallots or onion
¼ cup dry red wine
1 cup Brown Sauce (see recipe)
1 tablespoon cognac
1 teaspoon minced parsley

Have the butcher crack the bone; carefully remove the marrow. (You need about 3 tablespoons.) Dice it, and place in lukewarm water for 5 minutes, then drain.

Cook the shallots and wine for 5 minutes. Stir in the Brown Sauce and cognac; cook over low heat 10 minutes. Add the marrow and parsley just before serving. Heat. Taste for seasoning. Serve with steak or roast beef.

Makes about 1¼ cups.

SAUCE BIGARADE

½ cup boiling water
4 tablespoons grated orange rind
3 tablespoons minced shallots or onion
½ cup dry red wine

1½ cups Brown Sauce (see recipe)
½ cup orange juice
1 tablespoon red currant jelly
2 tablespoons Grand Marnier or Curaçao

Pour the boiling water over the rind, and let soak 5 minutes. Drain.

Cook the shallots in the wine until wine is reduced to half; stir in the Brown Sauce, orange juice, jelly, and liqueur. Cook over low heat 10 minutes, stirring frequently. Add the orange rind. Serve with duck or game birds.

Makes about 2 cups.

SAUCE FINES HERBES

2 teaspoons mixed dried herbs (tarragon, chervil, chives, thyme)
½ cup dry sherry

1½ cups Brown Sauce (see recipe)
⅛ teaspoon lemon juice
2 teaspoons butter
1 tablespoon minced parsley

Cook the herbs and wine until wine is reduced to half; strain. Add to the Brown Sauce with the lemon juice. Cook over low heat 5 minutes. Stir in the butter and parsley until butter melts. Serve with eggs or fish.

Makes about 1¾ cups.

SAUCE POIVRADE

2 tablespoons olive oil
⅓ cup minced onion
¼ cup grated carrot
3 tablespoons minced parsley
½ cup dry red wine

¼ cup wine vinegar
2 cups Brown Sauce (see recipe)
Dash ground cloves
¼ teaspoon freshly ground black pepper

Heat the oil in a saucepan; sauté the onion, carrot, and parsley for 5 minutes. Add the wine and vinegar, cooking until liquid is reduced to half. Add the Brown Sauce; cook over low heat 30 minutes. Strain the sauce, and return to a clean saucepan; stir in the cloves and the pepper. Cook over low heat for 5 minutes. Serve with any game.

Makes about 2¼ cups.

SAUCE VENISON

2 cups Sauce Poivrade
  (see recipe)
1 teaspoon lemon juice

3 tablespoons currant jelly
3 tablespoons heavy cream

Combine all the ingredients in a saucepan. Heat. Serve with venison.

Makes about 2¾ cups.

SAUCE MADÈRE

¾ cup Madeira or
  Amontillado sherry
2 teaspoons beef extract

1 cup Brown Sauce
  (see recipe)
1 tablespoon cognac
2 tablespoons butter

Cook the wine until reduced to half; stir in the beef extract and Brown Sauce. Cook over low heat 5 minutes. Add the cognac, and then the butter, stirring only until butter is melted. Serve with broiled meats or roast veal.

Makes about 1½ cups.

PERIGUEUX SAUCE

Sauce Madère (see recipe)	¼ cup chopped truffles

Combine the Sauce Madère and truffles. Heat. Serve with pheasant, guinea hen, partridge, or beef.

Makes about 1½ cups.

SAUCE PORTUGAISE

2 tablespoons minced
  shallots or onion
2 tablespoons butter
½ cup dry red wine

½ cup peeled, diced
  tomatoes
1 cup Brown Sauce
  (see recipe)
1 teaspoon tomato paste

Sauté the shallots in the butter for 5 minutes. Add the wine, and cook until wine is reduced to half. Stir in the tomatoes, Brown Sauce, and tomato paste. Cook over low heat 15 minutes. Taste for seasoning. Serve with poultry or beef.

Makes about 1½ cups.

SAUCE CHASSEUR

3 tablespoons butter
½ pound mushrooms, sliced
4 tablespoons minced
    shallots or onion
½ cup dry white wine
1½ cups Brown Sauce
    (see recipe)

2 tablespoons tomato paste
¼ teaspoon freshly ground
    black pepper
1 tablespoon minced
    parsley

Melt 2 tablespoons of the butter in a saucepan; sauté the mushrooms 5 minutes. Add the shallots, and sauté 2 minutes longer. Stir in the wine, and cook over low heat until wine is reduced to half. Add the Brown Sauce, tomato paste, and pepper. Cook 5 minutes. Blend in the remaining butter and the parsley. Serve with chicken, veal, or beef.

Makes about 1½ cups.

BÉARNAISE SAUCE

3 tablespoons tarragon
    vinegar
¾ cup dry white wine
2 peppercorns
1 tablespoon finely chopped
    shallots or onion
1 tablespoon finely chopped
    fresh tarragon, or 1
    teaspoon dried

1 tablespoon finely chopped
    fresh chervil, or 1
    teaspoon dried
3 egg yolks
½ teaspoon salt
1 cup melted butter
2 teaspoons minced
    parsley
Dash cayenne pepper

Combine the vinegar, wine, peppercorns, shallots, tarragon, and chervil in a sauce pan; cook over low heat until reduced to half. Beat the egg yolks and salt in a bowl; gradually add the wine mixture, beating steadily to prevent curdling. Gradually add the butter, beating steadily until the mixture is the consistency of very thick cream. Place over hot water, and beat for 1 minute. Strain, and add the parsley and cayenne pepper. If fresh herbs are used, add 1 teaspoon more of each before serving. Serve with beef or fish.

Makes about 1½ cups.

Variation:

SAUCE VALAISE

Add 1 teaspoon *glace de viande* or meat extract to the Béarnaise Sauce. Serve with broiled chicken or eggs.

HOLLANDAISE SAUCE

¼ pound (1 stick) sweet butter	¼ teaspoon salt
	1 tablespoon lemon juice
4 egg yolks	2 tablespoons heavy cream

Divide the butter into 3 pieces. With a wooden spoon, beat the egg yolks, salt, and lemon juice in the top of a double boiler. Place over hot, not boiling, water. Add 1 piece of butter and cook, stirring constantly, until butter melts. Add another piece of butter, and stir constantly until butter is absorbed. Add the last piece of butter, and stir until thickened. Be sure water does not boil.

Remove from the heat and blend in the cream. Serve as soon as possible. Serve with fish or vegetables.

Makes about 1¼ cups.

SALSA AMARILLA
EGG SAUCE

6 hard-cooked eggs	¼ teaspoon white pepper
¼ cup sweet sherry	½ teaspoon dry mustard
2 tablespoons olive oil	2 tablespoons chicken broth
1 tablespoon white vinegar	or water
½ teaspoon salt	

Separate the yolks and whites of the eggs. Force the whites through a sieve. Mash the yolks; mix in the sherry, then the oil, drop by drop. Blend in the vinegar, salt, pepper, mustard, broth, and egg whites. Serve with fish dishes.

Makes about ¾ cup.

SAUCE ESTRAGON
TARRAGON WINE SAUCE

4 tablespoons butter
3 tablespoons flour
2 cups milk, scalded
½ teaspoon salt
¼ teaspoon white pepper
1 cup dry white wine

3 tablespoons minced green onions
4 tablespoons minced fresh tarragon, or 1 tablespoon dried
3 tablespoons minced parsley

Melt 2 tablespoons of the butter in a saucepan. Blend in the flour, and cook, stirring over low heat until frothy. Do not let brown. Remove from the heat and let stand until mixture stops bubbling. Add the milk, beating with a wire whisk. Cook over low heat, beating steadily to the boiling point, then cook 5 minutes longer. Season with the salt and pepper.

In a saucepan, combine the wine, minced green onions, and tarragon. Bring to a boil and cook over medium heat until reduced to about 3 tablespoons. Strain into the white sauce; cook over low heat 2 minutes. Taste for seasoning. Just before serving, blend in the remaining butter and the parsley. (If fresh tarragon is used, add more tarragon in place of the parsley.) Serve with fish, vegetables, eggs, or chicken.

Makes about 2 cups.

SUGO DI CARNE
MEAT SAUCE (WITH WHITE WINE)

3 dried mushrooms
2 tablespoons butter
¾ cup chopped onion
½ cup grated carrot
3 tablespoons minced
　parsley
¾ pound ground beef

1 tablespoon flour
1½ teaspoons salt
½ teaspoon freshly ground
　black pepper
2 teaspoons tomato paste
1½ cups dry white wine
1 cup beef broth

Wash the mushrooms, cover with water, and let soak 15 minutes. Drain and slice.

Melt the butter in a saucepan; sauté the onion, carrot, and parsley 5 minutes. Add the meat and mushrooms; cook over medium heat, stirring almost constantly until browned. Blend in the flour, salt, and pepper, then the tomato paste. Add the wine and broth. Cook over low heat 45 minutes, stirring frequently. Taste for seasoning. Serve with *pasta*, or use as a sauce for meat.

Makes about 3 cups.

MEAT SAUCE (WITH RED WINE)

1 pound ground beef
2 tablespoons flour
4 tablespoons olive oil
¾ cup chopped onion
¼ cup grated carrot
3 tablespoons minced
　parsley
1½ cups dry red wine

1 16-ounce can Italian-
　style tomatoes
1½ cups beef broth
¾ cup chopped mushrooms
1½ teaspoons salt
½ teaspoon freshly ground
　black pepper
½ teaspoon basil

Toss the beef with the flour. Heat the oil in a saucepan; sauté the onion, carrot, and parsley 10 minutes. Add the beef; cook until browned, stirring frequently to prevent lumps from forming. Mix in the wine; cook over high heat 5 minutes. Add the tomatoes, broth, mushrooms, salt, pepper, and basil. Cook over low heat 1½ hours. Taste for seasoning. Serve with *pasta* or with meat dishes.

Makes about 3 cups.

SALSA DI FEGATINI
CHICKEN-LIVER SAUCE

5 dried mushrooms
1 pound chicken livers
3 tablespoons flour
4 tablespoons butter
1 teaspoon salt
¼ teaspoon freshly ground
  black pepper

½ cup Marsala or sweet
  sherry
1¼ cups chicken broth
2 tablespoons minced
  parsley

Wash the mushrooms, cover with warm water, and let soak 15 minutes. Drain and chop.

Wash the livers, remove any discolored areas, and dry. Dice the livers and toss with the flour.

Melt the butter in a saucepan; sauté the livers and mushrooms 5 minutes. Stir in the salt, pepper, and wine; cook over medium heat 5 minutes. Add the broth; cook over low heat 20 minutes. Mix in the parsley, and taste for seasoning. Serve with *pasta,* or use as a sauce for roast beef or steak.

Makes about 2½ cups.

SALSA ALLA GENOVESE
GENOVESE SAUCE

6 dried mushrooms
  (Italian, if available)
¼ cup olive oil
1½ pounds ground chuck
¾ cup chopped onion
2 cloves garlic, minced
½ cup chopped celery
½ cup grated carrot

2 teaspoons salt
½ teaspoon freshly ground
  black pepper
2 bay leaves
2 cups dry red wine
1 6-ounce can tomato paste
2 cups hot beef broth

Wash the mushrooms, cover with warm water, and let soak 10 minutes. Drain, and chop the mushrooms.

Heat the oil in a heavy saucepan; add the meat, and cook over high heat until browned, stirring frequently to prevent lumps from forming. Reduce heat; add the onion, garlic, celery, and carrot. Cook until browned. Mix in the mushrooms, salt, and pepper; cook 5 minutes. Add the bay leaves and wine, and bring to a boil. Stir in the tomato paste mixed with 1 cup of the broth. Cover, and cook over low heat 2½ hours, adding some of the remaining broth from time to time. Taste for seasoning. Discard the bay leaves. Serve on any *pasta,* or as a sauce for roast meat.

Makes about 5 cups.

RAGU
BOLOGNESE SAUCE

2 tablespoons butter	1½ tablespoons tomato paste
¼ pound ham, cut julienne	1¼ cups dry white wine
¾ cup chopped onion	1 cup water
¼ cup chopped celery	1 teaspoon salt
½ cup grated carrot	½ teaspoon freshly ground
¾ pound ground beef	black pepper
½ pound chicken livers,	⅛ teaspoon nutmeg
diced	1 cup heavy cream

Melt the butter in a saucepan; sauté the ham, onion, celery, and carrot 10 minutes, stirring frequently. Add the beef; cook over medium heat, stirring almost constantly, until browned. Stir in the livers; cook 2 minutes. Blend in the tomato paste, then stir in the wine, water, salt, pepper, and nutmeg. Cover, and cook over low heat 45 minutes, stirring frequently. Stir in the cream. Taste for seasoning. Serve with *pasta,* or use as a sauce for meat.

Makes about 3 cups.

ANCHOVY BUTTER SAUCE

1 tablespoon capers	¼ pound butter
1 tablespoon anchovy paste	1 teaspoon lemon juice
¼ cup dry sherry	2 teaspoons minced parsley

Rinse the capers under cold water; drain and chop.

Combine the anchovy paste with the sherry and butter in a saucepan; bring to a boil, and cook over low heat 10 minutes. Mix in the capers, lemon juice, and parsley; taste for seasoning. Serve with fish.

Makes about ¾ cup.

SHERRY-ROQUEFORT CHEESE DRESSING

1 egg
4 teaspoons sugar
1 tablespoon salt
5 cups salad oil
⅔ cup cider vinegar

1 clove garlic, minced
½ pound Roquefort cheese,
    diced
⅔ cup dry sherry

Beat the egg, sugar, and salt; gradually add the oil and half the vinegar, beating steadily. Stir in the garlic and cheese. Add the sherry and remaining vinegar, mixing until well blended. Chill until needed.

Serve on romaine, raw spinach, chickory, escarole, or a combination of greens. Be sure the greens are dry before adding dressing.

Makes about 1½ quarts.

Desserts

DEEP-DISH APPLE PIE

8 cups peeled, sliced apples
2 tablespoons flour
½ cup sugar
¾ cup sweet sherry

1 teaspoon cinnamon
1 tablespoon lemon juice
2 tablespoons butter
Pastry for 1-crust pie

Toss the apples with the flour, and combine in a saucepan with the sugar, sherry, cinnamon, and lemon juice. Bring to a boil, and cook over medium heat 10 minutes. Drain almost all the liquid. Taste apples for sweetness, and add a little more sugar if necessary. Cool 10 minutes.

Spread the apples in a deep 9-inch pie plate. Dot with the butter. Roll out the pastry and cover the pie plate with it. Make a slit in the top. Bake in a preheated 400° oven 25 minutes, or until the pastry is golden brown. Serve warm or at room temperature.

Serves 6-8.

Serve with a sweet German white wine, a sweet white Bordeaux, or with champagne.

FRAISES AUX CHAMPAGNE
STRAWBERRIES IN CHAMPAGNE

4 cups strawberries, washed
and hulled
¾ cup sugar
4 tablespoons kirsch (clear
cherry brandy)

1 cup champagne
2 cups whipped cream
¼ cup slivered blanched
toasted almonds

Place the strawberries in a bowl. Sprinkle with the sugar. Toss lightly but thoroughly. Add 2 tablespoons of the kirsch, and the champagne. Chill for 2 hours.

Add the remaining kirsch to the whipped cream. Mix

the strawberries in the bowl lightly, and divide among individual serving dishes. Cover with the whipped cream, and sprinkle the almonds on top.

Serves 6-8.

Serve with champagne, a sweet Bordeaux, or a sweet German white wine.

CHERRIES IMPERIAL

2 cups fresh or canned pitted black sweet cherries	1½ envelopes (1½ tablespoons) gelatin
⅓ cup sugar	1½ cups dry white wine
½ cup cognac	1 tablespoon lemon juice
	Blanched toasted almonds

Sprinkle the cherries with the sugar. (Use only ¼ cup for canned cherries.) Cover, and chill 1 hour. Drain the juice into a measuring cup. Add the cognac and enough water to make 1 cup.

Soften the gelatin in ½ cup of the wine. Place over hot water, and stir until dissolved. Mix in the remaining wine, the cherry liquid, and the lemon juice. Using half the mixture, spoon into eight custard cups. Chill until set. Put an almond in each cherry and arrange over the set gelatin. Cover with the remaining gelatin mixture. Chill until set. Unmold, and serve with whipped cream.

Serves 8.

Serve with champagne, a sweet white Bordeaux, a sweet German wine, or a sweet Italian white wine like Lacrima Christi.

PEACHES IN WINE SYRUP

2 pounds freestone peaches	1 tablespoon lemon juice
½ cup water	2 teaspoons grated lemon
1½ cups dry white wine	rind
¾ cup sugar	Currant jelly

Wash the peaches, plunge them into boiling water, then peel. Cut in half and discard the pits.

Bring the water, wine, and sugar to a boil. Add the peaches, lemon juice, and rind. Cover, and cook over low heat 10 minutes, or until peaches are tender but firm. Remove the peaches and arrange in a serving dish, cut side up. Cook the liquid over medium heat until syrupy. Cool. Place a teaspoon of jelly in each peach half, and pour the syrup over them. Chill.

Serves 6-8.

Serve with champagne, a sweet white Bordeaux, or a sweet German white wine.

STUFFED BAKED PEACHES

6 large firm freestone peaches	1 egg yolk, beaten
2 tablespoons sugar	1 tablespoon cognac
¾ cup macaroon crumbs	1 cup Marsala or sweet sherry

Peel the peaches, cut in half, and remove the pits. Scoop out a little of the pulp. Mash the pulp.

Cream the butter and sugar together; mix in the crumbs, peach pulp, egg yolk, and cognac. Stuff the peaches. Arrange in a buttered baking dish, and pour the wine over them. Pour the water into the dish. Bake in a 350° oven 25 minutes, or until peaches are tender but still firm.

Serves 6.

Note: Canned cling peaches may be prepared in the same manner, but bake only 15 minutes.

Serve with a sweet white Bordeaux or with champagne.

AMBROSIA CUP

2 cups diced oranges	¾ cup sweetened pineapple juice
1½ cups diced bananas	¾ cup port
1 cup diced pineapple	1 cup fine-grated coconut

Combine all the ingredients, and chill 1 hour before serving.

Serves 8-10.

Serve with a sweet white Bordeaux or with champagne.

WINE BERRY MOUSSE

1 pint raspberries or strawberries	1½ envelopes (1½ tablespoons) gelatin
1½ cups dry white wine	¼ cup water
¾ cup sugar	1 cup heavy cream, whipped

Hull, wash, and drain the berries. Combine the wine and sugar in a saucepan. Cook over low heat, stirring steadily, until sugar melts. Add the berries. Bring to a boil again, then cook over low heat 1 minute. Drain the berries; return liquid to pan.

Soften the gelatin in the water, then stir into the hot liquid until dissolved. Add the berries. Chill until mixture thickens. Fold in the whipped cream. Turn into a lightly oiled 1½-quart mold. Chill until set. Carefully unmold. Garnish with whipped cream and berries, if desired.

Serves 6-8.

Serve with champagne, a sweet Bordeaux like Château d'Yquem, or a sweet German white wine.

CARAMEL APPLES

6 baking apples	6 tablespoons butter
1⅓ cups packed brown sugar	⅓ cup dry white wine
	2 tablespoons cognac

Wash and core the apples. Put a tablespoon of the brown sugar in each, then a tablespoon of butter. Arrange in a buttered baking dish.

Cook the wine, cognac, and remaining brown sugar 10 minutes, or until syrupy. Pour over the apples. Bake in a preheated 350° oven 35 minutes, or until apples are tender, basting frequently. Chill. Serve with whipped cream.

Serves 6.

Serve with a sweet Bordeaux, or a sweet German or Italian wine.

BAKED APPLES IN WINE

6 large firm apples	¼ cup sugar
6 tablespoons currant jelly	2 tablespoons butter
1 cup dry white wine	

Peel and core the apples. Place a tablespoon of jelly in each. Arrange the apples in a baking dish. Mix the wine with the sugar, and pour over the apples. Dot with the butter. Bake in a 375° oven 35 minutes, or until the apples are tender, basting frequently. Serve hot or cold.

Serves 6.

Serve with champagne, a sweet Bordeaux, or a sweet German wine.

BAKED STUFFED APPLES

4 tablespoons butter
½ cup packed brown sugar
1 teaspoon cinnamon
2 tablespoons cognac

½ cup chopped walnuts
6 large baking apples
¾ cup sweet sherry

Cream together the butter and brown sugar until light and fluffy. Stir in the cinnamon, cognac, and nuts.

Wash the apples, remove the core, and peel about 2 inches down. Fill the centers with the nut mixture. Arrange in a buttered baking dish. Pour the sherry over the apples. Bake in a 375° oven 35 minutes, or until the apples are tender, basting frequently. Serve hot or cold, with whipped cream if desired.

Serves 6.

Serve with champagne, a sweet German white wine, or a sweet white Bordeaux like Château d'Yquem.

APPLE HEDGEHOG

3 pounds apples
¾ cup sugar
¼ cup water
2 tablespoons lemon juice
1 envelope (tablespoon) gelatin

½ cup sweet sherry
3 drops red food coloring
½ cup sliced blanched almonds

Peel and core the apples, and cut in small pieces. Combine with the sugar, water, and lemon juice in a saucepan. Cook over low heat about 20 minutes, or until tender. Watch carefully to prevent scorching.

While the apples are cooking, soften the gelatin in the sherry. Stir into the cooked hot apples until dissolved.

Purée in a blender, or force through a sieve. Taste for sweetness, and mix in the coloring.

Rinse a round or melon mold with cold water, and turn the apple mixture into it. Chill until firm. Unmold, and stud all over with the almonds.

Serves 6-8.

Serve with champagne or a sweet Bordeaux.

POIRES AU VIN ROUGE
BAKED PEARS IN RED WINE

8 firm pears
1⅛ cups sugar

1 teaspoon vanilla extract
4 cups dry red wine

Peel the pears, but leave stem on. In a baking dish, mix together the sugar, vanilla, and wine. Arrange the pears in it. Cover the dish, and bake in a 350° oven 50 minutes, or until pears are tender but firm. Baste and turn pears frequently. Chill.

Serves 8.

Serve with champagne, or a sweet German or Italian white wine.

PRUNE WHIP WITH PORT

1 pound unsweetened
    prunes
¾ cup sugar
4 teaspoons cornstarch
1 cup port wine

1 cup heavy cream
2 tablespoons confectioners'
    sugar
¼ cup slivered blanched
    almonds

Wash the prunes, cover with water, and let soak overnight. Bring to a boil, add ½ cup of the sugar, and cook over low heat 25 minutes, or until prunes are tender. Drain, pit the prunes, and purée in a blender, or force through a sieve.

Return the prunes to the saucepan; add the cornstarch mixed with the wine and the remaining sugar. Cook over low heat, stirring steadily, until thickened. Cool.

Whip the cream, and fold half of it into the prune mixture. Turn into 6 serving dishes. Mix the remaining whipped cream with the confectioners' sugar, and spoon on top. Chill. Sprinkle with the almonds.

Serves 6.

Serve with port wine, a sweet Bordeaux, or a sweet German or Italian wine.

PRUNE AND APRICOT COMPOTE

1 pound prunes	⅓ cup sugar
½ pound dried apricots	1 lemon, thinly sliced
2 cups dry white wine	½ cup blanched almonds
1 cup water	

Wash the prunes and apricots. Soak in the wine mixed with the water for 1 hour, then bring to a boil. Add the sugar and lemon. Cook over low heat 15 minutes, or until fruit is almost tender. Add the almonds; cook 5 minutes longer. Cool.

Serves 4-6.

Serve with champagne, a sweet white Bordeaux, or a Loire Valley wine like Sancerre.

PLUM PUDDING

3 cups fresh fine bread crumbs	1 cup seedless raisins
⅔ cup firmly packed light brown sugar	¾ cup currants
	¼ cup chopped dates
¾ teaspoon salt	¼ cup chopped candied citron
¾ teaspoon cinnamon	¼ cup chopped candied orange peel
½ teaspoon nutmeg	
¼ teaspoon ground cloves	¼ cup chopped candied lemon peel
¾ cup dry red wine, heated	
6 eggs, beaten	½ cup chopped apples
⅓ cup beef fat (suet), ground	¼ cup cognac

To make the bread crumbs, trim sliced white bread. Break the bread into small pieces and run in blender, or force through a sieve.

Mix the bread, brown sugar, salt, cinnamon, nutmeg, and cloves. Add the heated wine, and let stand 15 minutes. Mix in the eggs and suet. Using your hand, mix in the fruits and cognac. Be sure the fruits are well distributed.

Turn into a greased 2-quart mold. Cover tightly with the lid or with aluminum foil. Pour hot water to a depth of 1-inch into a pot with a cover. Place a rack in the pot and put the mold on it. Cover the pot, and cook over low heat 6 hours, adding boiling water from time to time to maintain the water level. The plum pudding may be served at once, or may be kept for a month or two. Reheat in the same manner before serving. Serve with hard sauce. Serves 10-12.

Serve with champagne, port wine, a sweet Bordeaux, or a sweet German wine.

ZABAIONE
MARSALA CUSTARD

8 egg yolks	1 cup Marsala or sweet
½ cup fine granulated sugar	sherry

Zabaione may be prepared at the table in a chafing dish or on the range in a double boiler. In the top part, beat the egg yolks and sugar with a wire whisk until thick. Beat in the wine; place over hot water and beat until hot and very thick, but do not let boil. Spoon into tall glasses or sherbet cups, and serve immediately. Serve with lady fingers, if desired.
Serves 6-8.
Serve with champagne or a sweet Italian wine.

RICE-NUT DESSERT

1½ cups raw rice	¾ cup sugar
4 cups milk	¾ cup ground almonds
1 teaspoon salt	3 egg yolks, beaten
¾ cup Marsala or sweet sherry	

Wash the rice under cold running water. Drain. Combine with the milk and salt; let stand 1 hour. Add the Marsala. Bring to a boil, and cook over low heat 15 minutes. Cool 10 minutes, then mix in the sugar, almonds, and egg yolks. Turn into a buttered baking dish. Bake in a preheated 350° oven 20 minutes. Chill.

Serves 4-6.

Serve with champagne or a sweet white Bordeaux.

SHERRY BREAD SLICES

8 slices white bread	4 tablespoons butter
1 cup milk	½ cup honey
2 eggs, beaten	½ cup dry sherry

Trim the bread, and cut each piece in half. Soak in the milk 3 minutes, drain well, and dip in the beaten eggs.

Melt the butter in a skillet; lightly brown the bread in it. Arrange pieces in a buttered baking dish. Mix the honey with the sherry and pour over the bread. Bake in a 325° oven 20 minutes, or until glazed. Serve hot or cold.

Serves 4-6.

Serve with a sweet German white wine, a sweet white Bordeaux like Sauternes, or a sweet Italian white wine.

CHAMPAGNE BAVAROIS

1 envelope (tablespoon) gelatin	⅛ teaspoon almond extract
⅔ cup champagne	½ cup ground blanched almonds
4 egg yolks	2 cups heavy cream, whipped
¾ cup sugar	

Soften the gelatin in the champagne. Place over hot water, and stir until dissolved.

Beat the egg yolks; add the sugar and almond extract, beating until thick and light in color. Gradually add the gelatin mixture, beating constantly. Mix in the almonds; fold in the whipped cream thoroughly but lightly.

Pour into a lightly oiled 2-quart mold. Chill until set, about 4 hours. Carefully unmold and serve. If desired, brandied fruits may be used as a garnish.

Serves 6-8.

Serve with champagne, a sweet white Bordeaux, or a sweet German wine.

Index

Abbacchio al vermouth, 129
Agneau
  à la Rheims, 129
  au vin rouge, 130
Almond sauce, chicken in, 72
Anguilles, sauce vert, 57
Anitra arrostita, 93
Appetizers,
  artichokes à la Grecque, 20
  cheese balls, 19
  cheese sticks, fried, 19
  chicken liver mousse, 23
  crabmeat Lucullus, 15
  eggplant in oil, 20
  eggs, hunter's style, 22
  eggs amandine, 23
  eggs in wine, 21
  fondue, Swiss, 24
  lobster au gratin, 16
  marinated herring, 18
  mushroom caps, stuffed, 21
  oysters, baked, and crabmeat, 17
  oysters with seafood sauce, 17
  scallops Lutetia, 15
  shrimp
    cocktail with sherry sauce, 14
    in papers, 14
    soufflé, 13
    spiced, 14
  snails in garlic butter, 18
  wine-cheese toast, 24
Apples,
  baked, stuffed, 186
  baked in wine, 185
  caramel, 185
  pork chops and, 147
  and red cabbage in red wine, 164
Apricot and prune compote, 188

Aragosta fra diavolo, 47
Artichoke hearts, with chipped beef, 123
Artichokes,
  à la Grecque, 20
  Jerusalem, in white wine, 162
  with lamb in vermouth, 129
  mushrooms and, 166
  Roman style, 162
Asado de puerco, 142
Aspic, wine, with trout, 42
Aubergines à la Grecque, 20
Beans,
  baked in wine, 163
  green, Portuguese style, 163
  lima, in wine sauce, 164

Beef,
  birds, 117
  boeuf,
    à la mode, 110
    en daube, 110
  Bourguignon, 105
  braised, 114, 116
    in red wine, 105
  chipped, with artichoke hearts, 123
  fillet,
    marinated, 104
    with mushrooms, 103
    pan-roasted, 104
    with pâté, 101
    in port, 99
    sautéed, in Marsala, 100
    stuffed, 102
    in vermouth, 99
  Italian, in white wine, 101
  and macaroni casserole, 120
  in Madeira, 100

with parsley sauce, 115
pepper steak, 95
pot roast, Swedish, 115
and prunes with spaghetti, 119
in red wine, 105
rib roast in wine, 98
roast,
  Bordeaux style, 96
  marinated, 97
  marinated Italian style, 98
sliced, with chicken liver sauce,
  121
steak,
  Diane, 120
  grilled, Burgundy style, 95
  and kidney pie, 121
stew,
  Gascony style, 110
  languedoc style, 108
  marinated, 111
  peasant, 107
  with rice, 109
  Roman style, 113
Stroganoff, 118
tenderloin, Lyons style, 116
with white wine, 106
Billi bi, 35
Bisque,
de homard, 29
lobster, 29
shrimp-mushroom, 30
Boeuf,
à la Catalane, 109
en daube, 110
au Madére, 100
en miroton, 107
à la mode, 112
rôti à la Bordelaise, 96
Bouillabaisse Marseillaise, 32
Boulettes de fromage, 19
Bracioline di maiale al vino, 144
Bread,
sherry slices, 190
wine-cheese toast, 24

Cabbage,
in champagne, 165
red, and apples in red wine,
  164
in red wine, 165
Caciucco, 38
Cadera de toro, 116
Calf's foot stew, 160

Calf's liver,
in Marsala, 154
with onions and wine, 154
in red wine, 153
Canard,
au Grand Marnier, 88
aux olives, 90
Véronigue, 92
au vin rouge, 89
Caper sauce, Rock Cornish hens
  in, 85
Capon,
Bordeaux style, 86
in wine sauce, 87
Cappelli di funghi ripieni, 21
Carbonada Criolla, 112
Carbonnade, la, 108
Carciofi alla Romana, 162
Carne asado, 97
Casserole,
beef and macaroni, 120
chicken, 71
chicken and almond, 72
chicken-noodle, à la Reine, 71
duck, 93
fish, 41
fish, potato and rice, 41
lima beans and onions, 164
lobster with macaroni, 42
meat ball, 122
de poisson, 41
pork, roast, 148
sauerkraut, 148
sea food, mixed, 40
of venison, 152
Cassoulet, 132
Cauliflower in wine sauce, 166
Cazuela,
de mariscos, 40
de pescado, 41
Celery with champagne sauce,
  166
Champagne,
Bavarois, 190
cabbage in, 165
chicken in, 59
sauce,
  celery with, 166
  with ham and pineapple,
    141
  lobster in, 50
  roast lamb in, 129
  sauerkraut with, 170
Chàmpignons Bourguignon, 168

Chapon,
  Lucullus, 87
  sauté à la Bordelaise, 86
Cheese,
  balls, 19
  chicken and ham rolls, 79
  soup, 36
  sticks, fried, 19
Cherries,
  imperial, 183
  sour, with duckling, 91
Cherry sauce, Cornish hens in, 85
Chestnuts and mushrooms with
    sweetbreads, 157
Chicken,
  and almond casserole, 72
  in almond sauce, 72
  Basque style, 68
  with bread crumbs, 69
  breast of, and ham, 79
  broilers, stuffed, 77
  casserole, 71
  in champagne, 59
  cheese, and ham rolls, 79
  with dumplings, 76
  in egg sauce, 67
  fricassee, French, in white
    wine, 73
  fricassee, Italian, 74
  with fruit, 70
  liquored, 62
  Marengo, 65
  and mushrooms, 75
  with mushrooms in cream
    sauce, 75
  with peppers, 74
  pullet, braised in wine cream,
    64
  in red wine, 61
    hunter's style, 59
  in rice ring, 82
  sautéed with eggplant, 66
  in spicy sauce, 69
  stuffed,
    poached, 78
    in sherry, 63
  with tarragon, 67
  with tomatoes and olives, 66
  and vegetable stew, 77
  in white wine sauce, 61
  in wine, hunter's style, 64
  in wine sauce, 60
Chickenburger, 80
Chicken liver mousse, 23

Chicken livers,
  with chicken and olives, 80
  with chicken in white wine, 81
  and mushroom sauce with rice,
    82
Chicken liver sauce, 179
  with sliced beef, 121
Chicken-noodle casserole à la
    Reine, 71
Chou au champagne, 165
Choucroute aux champagne, 170
Choux-fleurs Bourguignon, 166
Chowder, mussel, 34
Cioppino, 31
Ciorba de ceapa, 26
Clam,
  broth, with tomato, 33
  soup,
    cream of, 34
    Italian style, 33
Coquilles Saint-Jacques, 51
  marinées, 52
Coq au vin blanc, 61
Coq au vin rouge, 61
Cornish hen,
  in caper sauce, 85
  in cherry sauce, 85
Costa di manzo al vino rosso, 98
Costolette d'agnello, 131
Côtes de porc aux pruneaux, 145
Côtes de veau aux herbes, 134
Crabmeat,
  Lucullus, 15
  and oysters, baked, 17
Crab soup,
  king, cream of, 36
  with tomato, 35
Cream,
  sauce,
    chicken with mushrooms in,
      75
    ham in, 140
    veal croquettes with, 138
Croquettes, veal with cream,
    138
Custard, Marsala, 189

Daube à la mode d'Avignon, 130
Delices d'Emmenthal, 19
Desserts,
  ambrosia cup, 184
  apple hedgehog, 186
  apple pie, deep dish, 182

apples,
  baked, stuffed, 186
  baked, in wine, 185
caramel, 185
apricot, prune and, compote, 188
champagne Bavarois, 190
cherries imperial, 183
Marsala custard, 189
peaches in wine syrup, 183
pears, baked in red wine, 187
plum pudding, 188
prune,
  and apricot compote, 188
  whip, with port, 187
rice-nut dessert, 189
sherry bread slices, 190
strawberries in champagne, 182
wine berry mousse, 185
Dressings, see Sauces and dressings
Duck,
  braised, with grapes, 92
  with olive sauce, 90
  casserole, 93
  with Grand Marnier, 88
  Long Island roast, 92
  and olives, 90
  in red wine, 89
  roast stuffed, 93
  and vegetables in red wine, 89
Duckling with sour red cherries, 91
Dumplings with chicken, 76

Eggplant,
  chicken sautéed with, 66
  in oil, 20
Eggs,
  amandine, 23
  hunter's style, 22
  in wine, 21
Entrecôte grillé charollais Bourguignonne, 95
Escalopes de veau à la Savoyarde, 136
Escargots à la Bourguignone, 18
Estouffat,
  de boeuf, l', 110
  Catalan, 107

Fegato di vitello,
  al Marsala, 154
  alla Veneziana, 154
Filet de boeuf,
  farci, 102
  pôelé, 104
Filet mignon,
  aux champignons, 103
  au porto, 99
Fillets,
  de maquereaux au vin blanc, 54
  de poisson en soufflé, 45
Filetto,
  al pâté, 101
  Siciliana, 100
Fish,
  anchovies with onions and spaghetti, 43
  baked, with macaroni, 43
  casserole, 41
    mixed seafood, 40
    with potato and rice, 40
  eels in green sauce, 57
  filets de poisson en soufflé, 45
  herring, marinated, 18
  mackerel in white wine, 54
  with olives, 54
  red snapper, stuffed, baked, 56
  salmon steak,
    baked, 55
    poached, 55
  salt cod in red wine, 57
  scallops, baked, 51
    broiled and marinated, 52
  seafood kabobs, 44
  shrimp,
    deviled, 53
    risotto, 52
  sole,
    baked fillet of, 45
    with mushroom-hollandaise sauce, 46
  soup,
    Italian style, 32
    Marseillaise style, 32
    San Francisco, 31
  stew,
    Burgundy, 39
    Leghorn, 38
    in white wine, 39
  trout with wine aspic, 42
  tuna, sherried, 55
Foie gras, mushrooms with, 167

Foie de veau au vin rouge, 153
Fondue, Swiss, 24
Fraises aux champagne, 182
Fricadelles de veau à la crème, 138
Fricassee au vin blanc, 73
Fruit,
    with chicken, 70
    meat and, stew, South American style, 112
    soup, 37
    see also names of fruits

Gallina con arroz, 82
Garlic butter, snails in, 18
Grand Marnier with duck, 88
Grapes, braised duck with, 92
Gratin d'homard, 16
Green peppers, stuffed, 169
    in white wine, 168
Green sauce, eels in, 57
Grytstek, 115
Goulash, three-meat, 124

Hachua, le, 114
Ham,
    and breast of chicken, 79
    with champagne sauce and pineapple, 141
    with chicken and cheese rolls, 79
    in cream sauce, 140
    marinated, fresh, 140
    mousse, 139
    sliced, sautéed in Madeira, 139
    with sweetbreads and mushrooms, 157
Haricots verts Portugaise, 163
Hassenpfeffer, 161
Herbs, veal chops, with, 134
Herengs marinés, 18
Herring, marinated, 18
Homard,
    à l'Americaine, 47
    au champagne, 51
    à la Newburg, 49
    au porto, 49

Jambon,
    au ananas, 141
    à la crème, 140

Kabobs, seafood, 44
Käsebrötchen, 24
Kidneys, braised, 160
Kidney and steak pie, 121
King crab soup, cream of, 36
Kzartma, 126

Lamb,
    with artichokes and vermouth, 129
    chops in white wine, 131
    leftover, in white wine sauce, 131
    roast,
        in champagne sauce, 129
        crown of, 125
        leg of, 124
        marinated, 125
        saddle of, 126
    in red wine, 130
    shanks of, Near East style, 126
    shish kabob, 127
        Armenian, 128
    in sour-cream sauce, 128
    stew, in red wine, 130
Lima beans,
    and onion casserole, 164
    in wine sauce, 164
Liver,
    calf's, in Marsala, 154
    calf's, with onions and wine, 154
    calf's, in red wine, 153
Lobster,
    Americaine, 47
    bisque, 29
    casserole, with macaroni, 42
    in champagne sauce, 50
    au gratin, 16
    Newburg, 49
    in port, 49
    in spicy sauce, 48
    thermidor, 50
    in tomato sauce, 47
Lomo,
    con jerez, 144
    de toro, 104
Luk awaliani, 123

Macaroni,
    with baked fish, 43
    beef and, casserole, 120
Madeira,
    beef in, 100

sliced ham sautéed in, 139
Maiale marinato, 140
Manzo,
    brasato, 105
    in salsa di prezzemola, 115
Marsala,
    beef filet sautéed in, 100
    calf's liver in, 154
Matelote, 39
Meat,
    cassoulet, 132
    and fruit stew, South American style, 112
    goulash, three-meat, 124
    meat ball casserole, 122
    meat loaf, sausage, 153
    pie, Lorraine style, 149
    sauce, tripe in, 159
    stew, braised, Catalan style, 107
    Swiss steak, in wine sauce, 117
Meat-stuffed onions, Syrian style, 123
Morue en vin rouge, 57
Mousse,
    chicken liver, 23
    de foie de volaille, 23
    ham, 139
    au jambon, 139
    wine berry, 185
Mushroom,
    caps, stuffed, 21
    shrimp and, bisque, 30
    soup, cream of, 27
Mushrooms,
    and artichokes, 166
    beef fillet with, 103
    and chestnuts with sweetbreads, 157
    and creamed sweetbreads, Lucullus, 155
    with foie gras, 167
    ham and sweetbreads, 157
    with sautéed sweetbreads, 155
    sautéed in wine, 167
    in wine butter, 168
Mushroom-wine sauce, tongue with, 151
Mussel,
    chowder, 34
    soup, cream of, 35

Noodles, with Stroganoff sauce, 119

Nut-rice dessert, 189

Obstsuppe, 37
Oeufs à la Bourguignonne, 21
Oiseax de veau, 136
Olives,
    black, French veal and, 137
    with duck, 90
    pork chops with, 146
    sauce,
        with braised duck, 90
        tongue in, 152
Onion,
    lima beans and, casserole, 164
    soup,
        creamed, 26
        Rumanian, 26
Onions,
    minced pork and, 147
    stuffed with meat, Syrian style, 123
    and wine, with calf's liver, 154
Oxtails,
    in red wine, 158
    stew, 159
Oxtail soup, 28
Oysters,
    and crabmeat, baked, 17
    with seafood sauce, 17

Parsley,
    coating with roast pork, 143
    sauce, with beef, 115
Pâté, beef filet with, 101
Peaches,
    stuffed, baked, 184
    in wine syrup, 183
Pears, baked in red wine, 187
Peppers,
    green,
        stuffed, 169
        in white wine, 168
    veal and, 135
Pie,
    apple, deep dish, 182
    meat, Lorraine style, 149
Pineapple with ham in champagne sauce, 141
Plum pudding, 188
Pochouse Bourguignonne, la, 39
Poires au vin rouge, 187
Poisson aux olives, 54
Pollo,
    alla cacciatora, 59
    al cazador, 64

con frutas, 70
con funghi, 75
à la manchega, 77
con pan, 69
con peperoni, 74
piquante, 69
en salsa de almendras, 72
en salsa de huevos, 67
en salsa de vino, 60
alla Siciliana, 66
Pork,
  chops,
    and apples, 147
    with olives, 146
    pizzaiola, 145
    with prunes, 145
    in wine, 144
  loin,
    marinated, 141
    with sherry, 144
  minced, and onions, 147
  roast,
    casserole, 148
    marinated, 142
    with parsley coating, 143
    spiced, 143
  sauerkraut casserole, 148
  and sausages in wine, 150
  see also Spareribs
Port,
  beef filet in, 99
  lobster in, 49
Potatoes, festive, 169
Pot Roast, Swedish, 115
Poularde,
  Basquaise, 68
  à l'estragon, 67
Poulet,
  en casserole, 71
  au champagne, 59
  financiére, 80
  Marengo, 65
  à la Niçoise, 66
  nivernais, 76
Poultry, see Chicken; Duck;
  Squabs
Prune and apricot compote, 188
Prunes,
  beef and, with spaghetti, 119
  with pork chops, 145
Puchero de gallina, 78
Pudding, plum, 188
Puerco horneado, 143
Pullet, braised in wine cream, 64

Queue de boeuf, 158

Rabbit, marinated, 161
Ragoût,
  de boeuf Bordelaise, 111
  de queue de boeuf, 159
Ragu, 180
Red raspberry soup, cold, 37
Red wine,
  beef in, 105
    braised, in, 105
  cabbage in, 165
  calf's liver in, 153
  chicken in, 61
    hunter's style, 59
  duck in, 89
    and vegetables in, 89
  lamb stew in, 130
  oxtails in, 158
  red cabbage and apples in, 164
  salt cod in, 57
  squabs in, 84
  veal stew in, 137
Restes de gigot à la brissac, 131
Rice,
  with beef stew, 109
  with chicken livers and mush-
    room sauce, 82
  ring, chicken in, 82
Rice-nut dessert, 189
Risotto di scampi, 52
Ris de veau,
  Lucullus, 155
  au marrons, 157
  au vin blanc, 156
Rôti de porc,
  pôelé, 148
  Provençale, 143

Sauces and dressings,
  amarilla salsa, 176
  anchovy butter, 180
  Bearnaise, 175
  bigarade, 173
  Bolognese, 180
  Bordelaise, 172
  brown, 171
  chasseur, 175
  chicken liver, 179
  Duxelles, 171
  egg, 176
  estragon, 177

fines herbes, 173
Genovese, 179
Hollandaise, 176
Lyonnaise, 172
Madére, 174
meat,
    with red wine, 178
    with white wine, 178
mushroom, 171
Périgueux, 174
poivrade, 173
Portugaise, 174
Rouennaise, 172
salsa di fegatini, 179
sherry-Roquefort cheese, 181
sugo di carne, 178
tarragon and wine, 177
Valaise, 176
venison, 174
Sauerkraut,
    casserole, 148
    with champagne, 170
Sausage,
    meat loaf, 153
    and pork, in wine, 150
Scallops,
    baked, 51
    broiled and marinated, 52
    Lutetia, 15
    shrimp and, soup, 30
Seafood sauce, with oysters, 117
Sherried tuna, 55
Sherry,
    bread slices, 190
    chicken stuffed in, 63
    with roast loin of pork, 144
    sauce, with shrimp cocktail, 14
Shish Kabobs, 127
    Armenian, 128
Shrimp,
    cocktail, with sherry sauce, 14
    deviled, 53
    and mushroom bisque, 30
    in papers, 14
    risotto, 52
    and scallop soup, 30
    soufflé, 13
    spiced, 14
Snails in garlic butter, 18
Sopa de pescado, 30
Soufflé,
    filets de poisson en, 45
    shrimp, 13
Soups,
    cheese, 36

chicken-in-the-pot, Belgian, 27
clam,
    broth, with tomato, 33
    cream of, 34
    Italian style, 33
cold red raspberry, 37
crab,
    king, cream of, 36
    with tomato, 35
fish,
    Italian style, 32
    Marseille style, 32
    San Francisco, 31
fruit, 37
German wine, 28
lobster bisque, 29
mushroom, cream of, 27
mussel,
    chowder, 34
    cream of, 35
onion,
    creamed, 26
    Rumanian, 26
oxtail, 28
shrimp,
    mushroom bisque, 30
    and scallop, 30
tomato,
    broth, with clams, 33
    with crab, 35
    with wine, 29
Sour cream, veal rump rolled
    with, 133
Sour-cream sauce, lamb in, 128
Spaghetti,
    beef and prunes with, 119
    onions and anchovies, with, 43
Spareribs, Hawaiian-Chinese, 150
Spezzato,
    di maiale, 147
    di pollo, 81
Spiced roast pork, 143
Spicy sauce,
    with chicken, 69
    with lobster, 48
Squabs,
    with peas, 83
    in red wine, 83
    stuffed, 84
Steak au poivre, 95
Stew,
    beef,
        Gascony style, 110
        languedoc style, 108
        marinated, 111

peasant, 107
  with rice, 109
  Roman style, 113
braised, Catalan style, 107
calf's foot, 160
chicken and vegetable, 77
fish,
  Burgundy, 39
  Leghorn, 38
  in white wine, 39
lamb, in red wine, 130
meat and fruit, South American style, 112
oxtail, 159
veal, in red wine, 137
Stroganoff sauce, with noodles, 119
Stufatino alla Romana, 113
Stufato di manzo, 106
Sweetbreads,
  with chestnuts and mushrooms, 157
  creamed, and mushrooms, Lucullus, 155
  ham and mushrooms, 157
  sautéed, with mushrooms, 155
  in white wine, 156
Swiss fondue, 24
Swiss steak, in wine sauce, 117

Tarragon with chicken, 67
Toast, wine-cheese, 24
Tomato,
  broth, with clams, 33
  sauce, with lobster, 47
  soup,
    with crab, 35
    wine, 29
Tongue,
  glazed, casserole, 151
  with mushroom-wine sauce, 151
  in olive sauce, 152
Tournedos Lyonnaise, 116
Tourte Lorraine, 149
Tranches de jambon aux Madère, 139
Tripe in meat sauce, 159
Trippa alla fiorentina, 159
Turkey, marinated stuffed, 87

Uova alla cacciatora, 22

Veal,
  birds in wine, 136
  chops,
    stuffed, 134
    with herbs, 134
  croquettes with cream, 138
  French, and black olives, 137
  leg, roast of, 133
  and peppers, 135
  rump, rolled with sour cream, 133
  stew in red wine, 137
  in vermouth sauce, 136
Vegetables with duck, in red wine, 89
Venison, casserole of, 152
Vermouth,
  beef fillet in, 99
  lamb with artichokes in, 129
Vermouth sauce, veal in, 136
Vitello con peperoni, 135

Waterzooi de poulet, 27
Weinsuppe, 28
White wine,
  artichokes, Jerusalem, in, 162
  with beef, 106
  chicken and livers in, 81
  fish stew in, 39
  in French fricassee, 73
  green peppers in, 168
  Italian beef in, 101
  lamb chops in, 131
  mackerel in, 54
  sauce,
    chicken in, 61
    lamb leftovers in, 131
  sweetbreads in, 156
Wine,
  aspic, with trout, 42
  chicken in, hunter's style, 64
  mushrooms sautéed in, 167
  and onions, with calf's liver, 154
  pork chops in, 144
  pork and sausages in, 150
  and tomato soup, 29
  veal birds in, 136
Wine butter, mushrooms with, 168
Wine cream, pullet braised in, 64

Wine sauce,
  capon in, 87
  chicken in, 60
  cauliflower in, 166
  Swiss steak in, 117

Zabaione, 189
Zuppa,
  di pesce, 32
  di vongole, 33